Start and Run a Profitable Bouncy Castle Hire Business

Please visit Author's page on Amazon for future updates on new releases.

Start and Run a Profitable
Bouncy Castle Hire Business

A complete step-by-step guide which reveals powerful insider-secrets, profit-multiplying strategies, tips and tricks of the trade to starting, running and growing a successful inflatable hire business and skyrocketing your personal wealth.

Mark Jerram

HAVERSHAM INTERNATIONAL

Published in 2018 by Haversham International Ltd
Printed by CreateSpace, an Amazon.com Company
Jacket Design: Ana Pavão

Copyright © Mark Jerram 2018

Mark Jerram has asserted his right to be identified as the author of this work under the Copyright, Designs, and Patents Act 1988.

All rights reserved. No part of this publication may be reproduced, stored in a retrieval system, or transmitted in any form or by any means, electronic, mechanical, photocopying, recording, or otherwise without the prior permission of the copyright owners. Short quotations are allowed for fair use for educational purposes only, or as permitted by the UK Copyright, Designs, and Patents Act 1988 and Section 107 or 108 of the United States Copyright Act 1976.

ISBN-13: 978-1546509912
ISBN-10: 1546509917

I dedicate this book to the
memory of my much-loved mother
Mrs Elizabeth Jerram (1936 - 2016)

Contents

FOREWORD VII

INTRODUCTION IX
    Why This Book? IX
    The History of Bouncy Castles X

PART ONE - YOUR PATH TO FINANCIAL FREEDOM 1
    The Opportunity - Why Now Is The Perfect Time For This Business 1
    How You Can Enjoy The Profits From Hiring Inflatables 5

WHY IS A BOUNCY CASTLE SO MUCH BETTER THAN OTHER CHILDREN'S PARTY ENTERTAINMENT? 11
    Take A Hard Look At Yourself 12
    Joining the BIHA 14
    Who Runs The BIHA Website, the two Facebook Groups and the Forum? .. 15
    How To Get Started 17
    Safecic.co.uk 19

EQUIPMENT NEEDED TO START UP YOUR BUSINESS 23
    Finding Your First Bouncy Castle To Buy 24
    Never buy 'TOY' Bouncy Castles to hire out 25
    A Note About Buying Second Hand Bouncy Castles And Inflatables 26
    If You Really Must Save Money and Buy Second Hand 26
    Types of inflatables to buy 28
    Adult Bouncy Castles 29
    Slides & Combos 29
    Obstacle Courses (Assault Courses) 30
    Safety Testing For Bouncy Castles 31
    Whom Do You Hire To? 34
    Safety 36
    Heath & Safety 36
    Public Liability Insurance 37
    Inflatable Testing 37

Method Statements & Risk Assessing..*38*
Demonstrating good inflatable hire practices................................*38*
BIHA and TIPE..*39*
Presenting a Professional Image..*40*
Launching Your Business..*44*
How To Track Enquiries..*46*

IDEAS FOR INFLATABLES FOR OLDER CHILDREN AND ADULTS AT PRIVATE PARTIES AND EVENTS **49**

How To Start Up The Right Way From Day One Running Your Business Part Time..*50*
Taking The Leap Into Full Time..*51*
How To Make Sure You Are In Profit From Day One..................*53*
Keeping Running Costs Under Control...*56*

START UP INFORMATION FOR COMPLETE BEGINNERS.................**59**

How To Ensure The Rain Does NOT Spoil The Bouncy Castle Party!.........*59*
Inflatable Hire Disaster Preparation Kit.......................................*61*
Promoting Additional Services..*62*

MORE ON SAFETY **65**

Compulsory..*67*
Strongly Recommended..*69*
The Law and 'Best Practice' for Operators of Inflatable Play Equipment...*70*
The scope of the BS EN 14960:2013 standard..............................*71*
Are Bad Telephone Practices Hurting Your Bouncy Castle Hire Business?.*75*

YOUR BUSINESS WEBSITE **77**

How To Skyrocket Your Bookings By Uploading Videos Of Your Bouncy Castles Onto YouTube.com...*82*
You Must Have A Mobile-friendly Website -But it can be the same site as your main website...*84*
Free Ways To Get More Business..*86*

ONLINE MARKETING **93**

82 OTHER BLUNDERS WHICH COULD DAMAGE YOUR BOUNCY CASTLE HIRE BUSINESS..**95**

35 CREDIBILITY FACTORS FOR YOUR BOUNCY CASTLE BUSINESS 99

PART TWO - 70 SURE-FIRE TIPS FOR SUCCESS IN THE INFLATABLES HIRE BUSINESS 107
    Build Trust and Credibility 108
    Traditional Marketing - Even More Tips 114
    Dealing with Customers 118

BOUNCY CASTLES DISASTERS AND LESSONS TO BE LEARNED FROM THEM! 133

BIHA TIPS OF THE WEEK..169

TIPS SHARED BY THE BIHA 211
    USEFUL INDUSTRY LINKS 216
    In Closing...218

BIHA MEMBERSHIP BENEFITS 219

Foreword

by Ken Jones

I have known Mark Jerram for more than thirty years and am pleased to count him as a friend and business colleague. He is friendly and always willing to help another business person or friend in need. He lives life honestly and with a positive code of personal ethics that makes others respect him.

Mark is also an experienced businessman who has become well known as an entrepreneur and successful marketer. One thing that separates Mark from many other business people I know is his willingness to help other people. Anyone who has had even a short conversation with him will know how open he is and how freely he gives help to anyone in the Inflatable hire business.

I recommend this book wholeheartedly, safe in the knowledge that both beginners and experienced business owners will reap significant benefits if they follow the enclosed guidelines carefully.

Ken Jones (Author and Publisher - KJPublishing.com)

Introduction

I first thought of writing this book fifteen years ago. It is the book I wished I had available when I set up my own Bouncy Castle Hire business in 1992.

Why This Book?
The inflatable hire business can potentially be a very profitable and enjoyable way of earning a good living. This book is the culmination of over 30 years of my own experience combined with that of thousands of members of the BIHA.

We have all made mistakes, and we have all had our successes. Is it not better to learn from others though? Why try to re-invent the wheel or discover the wheel in the first place? Far better to take the combined wisdom learnt through the hard work of others and take a shortcut to business success.

Read the tips in this book - some of them are virtually priceless. Highlight anything that seems to fit into your way of doing things. This is not a book to read and put on the shelf. Rather it is a working book. Then try to incorporate the ideas you like the best into your own business. Not all the tips will be relevant to you although it is hoped that some of the ideas and techniques will form a 'springboard' for you to develop further or customise your own business. You may not even agree with all these ideas, or you may be doing something in a different way which you feel works better for you or better suits your personality. No matter, just one tip in this book could make or save you the cover price many times over. In that sense, this book will probably be one of the best investments you will ever make for your business.

You may have seen some of these tips elsewhere, especially if you are a member of the BIHA (see resources). However, this report contains the best ideas (and the worst mistakes to avoid) in one place. This volume should be a continual source of reference for both the experienced hirer and the relative beginner. As I said before, one good idea taken from this report and put into practice may repay your annual membership fee many times over!

Finally, there might be a small degree of overlap or possibly even repetition in this book. This is inevitable to a degree. Business has many overlaps, and when dealing with such a large number of tips, it cannot be helped. I want all BIHA members and readers to be absolutely as successful as possible in their inflatable hire business.

The History of Bouncy Castles
In the late 1950s, former NASA employee, John Scurlock, was a mechanical engineer who was also interested in physics. His greatest legacy was the invention of the safety air cushion used by fire and rescue teams when rescuing people jumping from heights, particularly high buildings.

In 1959, Scurlock was experimenting with inflatable covers for use on tennis courts and swimming pools to protect them from the elements. His original intention was to create a cover that could protect tennis courts during sudden downpours, which could very quickly be removed after the had rain stopped, and easily folded and stored in a small place until the next time it was required.

One day he happened to notice his employees were having fun bouncing around on the cover he was currently testing. As he watched, he got the idea that children would enjoy bouncing around on something similar. He leased warehouse space in New Orleans and began manufacturing what he called Space Walks, a large air mattress specifically created for children. Later he added walls and a ceiling, and clear plastic windows. The surface was typically reinforced PVC and nylon, and the equipment was inflated using blowers with a gas such as helium, nitrogen, or hydrogen.

In 1968, as Scurlock's creation began to spark more interest, his wife Frances realized there was a limited market for the purchase of Space Walks as the price was prohibitive. However, she noted the family could make more money by renting them for events such as birthday parties, company picnics, school fetes, church socials, and other activities.

Later, their son Frank expanded the business throughout the USA under various brand names. He was also responsible for creating the first inflatable indoor play parks in Louisiana and Tennessee. As the hire business grew over the years, the Scurlocks invented a number of other inflatables such as tents, domes, and signs. Because the newer structures were enclosed, they created inflated columns that would support netting walls allowing air to pass through to help cool the inside.

There is some confusion as to where the bouncy castles were first developed. Some say they were created by university students in England as early as 1961, while others say the Scurlocks were responsible for the development of the castles.

PART ONE
Your Path To Financial Freedom

The Opportunity - Why Now Is The Perfect Time For This Business
Let me assure you from the outset that there is a huge opportunity for you in hiring out bouncy castles and other inflatables. You might think that the internet is full of competitors advertising bouncy castles for hire and it probably is. But I know from experience of running the British Inflatable Hiring Alliance (BIHA) that you can still start your own profitable business in a crowded marketplace.

My email inbox receives daily communications from people wanting to set themselves up with a bouncy castle hiring business. They have seen the opportunity, and if you are reading this page, then I know that you have as well.

There is, however, a correct way of going about setting up your business, and this book will be the key to your success. As the founder member of the BIHA, I invite you to join over 1,500 other inflatable hire companies who are BIHA members and who already make a good income for themselves. Instructions for joining the BIHA are in a later chapter but if you are in a hurry go to this website and get started right away, log on to www.biha.org.uk.

The bouncy castle hire business is a very easy business to get into. Sometimes it seems too easy. I have seen people think that they have a better idea of how to start up their business and yet they fail to make any money due to poor business decisions. We are specialists at helping people start out in this business. We know how you can set up your business and be making money from day one. We offer a simple solution to help you make money.

We have researched and found that when times are hard, hiring a bouncy castle to celebrate a birthday or any other special occasion, is still cheaper than the average party at an indoor play centre or a trip to the cinemas or local kart track! This is why bouncy castle rental is so popular and why it is a great business for you to set up and run from home.

Let us take a look exactly why this is a hot opportunity with four standard party examples:

> PARTY A - A Garden Party with a Bouncy Castle
> PARTY B - A Cinema trip Birthday Party
> PARTY C - An Indoor Play Centre Party
> PARTY D - A Go Karting Party

PARTY A - A Garden Party with a Bouncy Castle

The results showed that the cheapest alternative was Party A. A Garden Party with a Bouncy Castle hired in. The costs were as follows:

> 1 x bouncy castle hire = £60.00, with a complimentary bag of balloons and free party invitations for the guests.
>
> A small finger buffet was supplied as purchased from a well-known supermarket, as follows:-
>
> > 50 Pack of sausages rolls = £3.00
> > 2 White loafs = £2.20
> > Jar of Strawberry Jam = 50p
> > Pack of cheese = £2.50
> > 12 pack of crisps = £2.00
> > 2 x No Added Sugar Drinks = £2.10
> > Jelly = 40p
> > Value box of party cakes = £2.00
> > Jug of water = Nil
> > Total for buffet = £14.70

TOTAL COST OF PARTY A = £74.70

Here are some typical responses from parents who took their children to this party. (I have used a real bouncy castle party that I ran to price this example):

"Fun for the whole family to join in."
"Cheaper than any other type of kids' party."
"Great for getting the kids bouncing around and exercising - they didn't have to sit still for any length of time."
"Very good that hall hire is cheap and if the forecast was poor we could have the party indoors for just a bit more money."

PARTY B - A Cinema trip Birthday Party

Average cinema tickets for 12 children and one adult supervising = £60
Price checked with a national UK cinema chain in March 2018.

Drink and popcorn per child is not usually included in the price so you will probably need to budget about £5 per child = £60
Pizza later (approximately) = £32.00

TOTAL COST OF PARTY B = £152

Some typical quotes from parents on the Party B…

"My daughter got bored halfway through and was climbing over the chairs because she lost interest."
"Expensive and the children didn't get to play together, my eldest liked the film."
"My son was afraid of the bad guy in the movie and spent the whole time on my lap. My legs are still aching now."

The problem with cinema parties is that you will almost never find a film that will suit all the children. So as a parent you have the task of occupying bored and disengaged children.

PARTY C - An Indoor Play Centre Party

12 x £10 per child entry to the indoor soft play area

TOTAL COST OF PARTY C = £120

This price will usually include a box of food and a drink. To have exclusive use of the play centre would be around £199 for 2 hours at the weekend. (Pricing example taking from a play centre in Surrey).

Some quotes from parents on the Party:

"I would have preferred it if the party hadn't been so noisy. It was very busy in there."
"Too many children from other parties to make it fun for my child."
"I was a little anxious over the security issues, as the doors were open to let cool air in, and as it was open to the public anyone could walk in"

PARTY D - A Go Karting Party
This assumes that you can arrange a Go Karting party. At tracks, there is a minimum age restriction.

    1-hour party without food £200.00
    Pizza on the way home £32

TOTAL COST OF PARTY D = £232

Some quotes from parents on the Party:

"The heavy rain made the track very muddy so the children didn't get as many laps as they should have done."
"I was concerned about the safety issues with some of the boys driving very fast."
"There was no provision for children aged under four or over 10."

When you look at the facts and figures you can see why hiring bouncy castles will still remain popular for children's parties whatever the state of the nation's economy. The figures reiterate how literally anyone can enter the business and why you can continue to sustain a profit for many years to come. Bouncy castles are a lot of fun, and for parents looking at their stretched finances, it can be a viable and affordable option for a memorable celebration event.

How You Can Enjoy The Profits From Hiring Inflatables
Many people start up a bouncy castle hire business on their own without getting proper advice and support from others in the industry. However, this approach leaves them wide open to making mistakes that can harm their inflatable hire business and slow its growth.

By sharing information on common 'stumbling blocks', we hope that you can learn from mistakes others have made and thereby avoid some of the obstacles that many before you have had to overcome.

Here are some of the most common errors:

1. Starting without a proper plan. You need more than just lots of energy, enthusiasm and a willingness to work at weekends. It is important that you study the market in your town or city, your competition and develop a plan for how you are going to make money in the bouncy castle hire business.

If you find that there are lots of companies near you offering adult bouncy castle hire perhaps you should concentrate on hiring to children's events only. There are many other niche markets within the industry. If you can specialise in a specific niche and become known for expertise in that area of the business, you will likely get more leads.

An example of this might be bouncy castles for weddings. These bouncy castles are for the adults including the bride and groom. If you invest in a large adult sized bouncy castle and offered it specifically for weddings you may, over time, corner that market in your area. Other competitors will start giving you leads for wedding hires if they do not have a suitable inflatable to hire out.

Your competitors are not your enemies. In my business, over the years I built up working relationships with a large group of professional hire companies. We helped each other out and shared hiring events when there was a large local fete or fayre. How do you set these alliances up? You call them and tell them what you are thinking of doing and ask them if they join. It was contacts like these that formed the basis of what became the BIHA.

So do not make the mistake of not having a proper plan. And do not treat your competitors as your enemies. Most people in the industry are more than willing to cooperate with you.

2. Another simple error is calling your bouncy castle hire business a name that comes very low down in the alphabet. The reason why you should try and call your business with a name that starts with an 'A' or even a number is that most offline and online directories list bouncy castle companies alphabetically. If your business starts with a 'P' or worst case a 'Z' then you will be at the bottom of the listings. Most people looking to hire a bouncy castle will start at the top and go downwards. You could miss out on a huge amount of enquiries and bookings if you are listed near the end of an internet search query.

However, do not try and trick the search engines by calling your company AAAABouncycastles.com. They are wise to this trick now, and it will not help you. It might even get you blacklisted by the search engines.

3. Giving up your 'day job' too soon is something I see happening all the time! Although the bouncy castle hire business can be very lucrative, it is very important when you first start that you still continue to work in your normal job. As soon as your income from hiring bouncy castles reaches a point where you feel that you can comfortably live off it, then this is the point where it may be appropriate to start thinking of quitting your day job in order to focus 100% on hiring bouncy castles.

Do not be in a rush to make this step as some people's new business can be quite seasonal until they get a good number of regular customers and a name for good service. Being self-employed can be a rollercoaster ride at times, and you want to be 100% sure of your finances before making the leap. Having said this, knowing that you are in control of your days and your income is a thrill I would never give up. I could never go back to being employed by someone else.

4. Do not take on employees until your turnover hits a sufficient level. And definitely, do not take on your best friend to help you in your business. Friends are good for some things but not always for employing. Many people forget that hiring employees can be very expensive if there is insufficient work to go round. Sometimes it is better to use sub-contractors first although you should check with your accountant and lawyer as to how best to do this to ensure you comply with the relevant law.

The legal side of employing people is full of complications and procedures that you would hardly believe. This is particularly true in the area of health and safety. So if your business plan includes employees working for you, get some good advice from an expert.

5. Keeping employees because they are 'nice' and 'try hard' is not a good reason to retain them. It can be difficult to dismiss someone, but a bad employee or someone who is just not pulling their weight could drag your bouncy castle company down. Think about it this way; if you now had the opportunity to hire this person (knowing what you now know about their work habits) would you hire him or her? If not, it is time to be open with the employee and let him or her know they are not fit enough for your bouncy castle hire company.

Dismissing someone having worked with them closely is a tough time for both people. But your income and reputation are at stake here, and you cannot risk poor reviews and loss of trade just because you do not want to hurt someone's feelings.

6. Not diversifying or just hiring out small bouncy castles and inflatables for children's parties. Saturday night television has given people an appetite for adrenaline fuelled fun experiences. Your job is to try and help them enjoy themselves by hiring out appropriate equipment. More and more customers now want more than just a bouncy castle, e.g. they may want a slide, garden games, obstacle course, etc. If you cannot supply this

equipment, it may be a good idea to work with a competitor (or rent from a competitor) and then share the income. If you cannot provide these added services, your customers may switch to an inflatable hire company that can better meet their needs.

When a lead for business comes in, you do not want to say, "No," just because you do not own what they want to hire. If you have built an alliance with someone who has suitable, appropriate equipment, you can say, "Yes," and still make some additional income for each of you.

7. Not saying, "Thank You," often enough. This also includes smiling and looking like you are enjoying your work. Bouncy castle hire is part of the entertainment business, and you will not impress people if you walk around and set up your equipment looking like a misery.

So smile nicely and thank people for their business. Try and go the extra mile with them (within reason) and show yourself willing and able to help. Everyone likes to know they are appreciated. This includes your employees, your customers, your suppliers and anyone else who has helped you or given you advice that has helped your bouncy castle business grow.

8. Not visiting and participating in the online discussion Facebook group. Using the BIHA Facebook group **(facebook.com/groups/biha4u)** is like having a board of advisers or experts on tap who will help answer any questions, problems and issues you are facing. You do not have all the answers -even if you think you do. I have been in this business for 25 years, and I still come across questions and ideas that are completely new.

So do not live your life in a corner wondering what to do. Get on the forum and participate. After some experience, you will find that you can help other people who are starting up in business. That is a great feeling.

9. Concerning spending too much money. Do not blow your whole redundancy money or spare capital funds on one piece of equipment because it looks shiny and new. You might be investing in the wrong thing.

When you first start out resist the urge to invest in expensive equipment, fancy office furniture, or gadgets you do not need.

I knew a 'businessman' who set himself up in an expensive rented office with a top of the range computer, photocopier/scanner, expensive phone system and a big oak desk and told me he was running his own business. He even had a PA to do all his reception and typing work. The only problem was that he did not have any customers -none at all. He lost a huge redundancy payment in 18 months because he spent money on the wrong things. He should have spent his money on marketing and selling his service before paying for his office luxuries.

10. You can spend too little money. While you do not want to go overboard, you do need the right equipment and vehicles etc., so that you can deliver the hiring correctly. There is a basic amount of equipment and stock that you need in order to get started. Otherwise, your business will not be profitable.

Your bouncy castle hire business can be successful if you have the enthusiasm, the drive, the passion and the willingness to learn from other people's mistakes. Take your time, do your homework and learn from those who have already become successful.

Why Is A Bouncy Castle So Much Better Than Other Children's Party Entertainment?

To answer this question, we need to look at the other choices available when organising a children's party. There is a great deal of competition, and some of the options for parents are totally bewildering.

Traditional Children's Parties
Whilst no doubt you share the same happy memories as I do, of playing pass the parcel, musical chairs and the like, today's children tend to have higher expectations. Even though all the children who attend are likely to have a good time they are also likely to think such games a bit 'babyish' and that the party has been done 'on the cheap.' Children can be very cruel and no doubt some of your child's 'friends' will say so at some point. Although it is hard work keeping the children amused, on the positive side there is very little expense involved and the family will usually rally round to help with preparing the food.

Organised (Commercial) Parties
These parties come in all shapes and sizes. The current 'new boy on the block' is the trampoline party. There are commercial warehouses full of trampolines that host children's party. A child's meal is normally included and a good time is had by all. I assume the food is consumed after all the jumping around has been completed. Otherwise, it could get a bit messy! Unfortunately, all of this comes at a price, £20 per head or more! Unless you are willing to pay around £240 for the party, this means that only your child's immediate friends can be invited, not the whole class.

The other negative points are that:

1. The food may be too 'grown-up' for some children who could end up eating nothing.
2. Time spent in the play area is timed, and the children have to leave when their hour is up.
3. The play area may not be exclusive to your party. Other children or even other parties are likely to be sharing it with you.

Another current craze is paintball parties. Again these demand a large investment in comparison to the traditional party at home. There are restrictions for who can use the weapons and it is all over far too quickly.

These two modern examples show the problems faced by parents trying to give their children a memorable party event whilst at the same time not paying out something equivalent to a week's wages.

Bouncy Castle Parties
Other than the hire charge of the bouncy castle the costs are the same as for a traditional party. Like a traditional party, there is no need to be careful with the number of children attending so the whole class can be invited avoiding jealousy or bad feeling on the playground. Parents can still play party games with the children if they wish but there is no need to keep it up for the duration of the party, and there is a more relaxed feeling. Parents can sit in the garden and get to know one another whilst watching the children play. Basically, you have installed a soft play area in your own garden for the whole day at the cost of not much more than £2 per head!

Your only concerns may be the size of your garden or the weather. Garden suitability problems are not insurmountable! Whichever way you look at it bouncy castle hire makes a lot of sense! And what kid can resist jumping on a bouncy castle? Very few indeed!

Take A Hard Look At Yourself
Having hopefully convinced you that the inflatable hire industry is a multi-million-pound business and at the heart of it all are the hire companies and manufacturers/suppliers across the UK and the world, you need to consider if you are suitable as a person to take the leap and set up in business.

Think about the type of person you are and ask yourself some questions:

Why do you want to work for yourself?
Are you a self-starter who gets up in the morning and is motivated to do something? Couch potatoes do not make good business people.

Can you make decisions quickly and correctly? You need to make up your mind and take action. People who sit on the fence and cannot decide which way to turn do not work well without a boss checking up on them.

How do you receive criticism? Do you fight back with some arguments of your own or do you listen to what people tell you? You do not have to like being criticised, but you can always learn from it. I had a job 20 years ago that I did not give my full attention to. I messed it up badly, and the customer rightly called me and told me what he thought of me. I was furious with emotions inside, but I also knew that the customer was correct in his criticism. I accepted the criticism over the phone and offered to make good what I had done wrong. The customer was so astounded that he became a good source of new customers for many years afterwards!

I became a much better person through this episode and never made the same mistake again. Some people will never accept that they are in the wrong. If this is you then running a business is not a good idea for you.

Are you fit and healthy? Running a business is arduous physically and often surprises new business people. Add to this the carrying around of the bouncy castles and other equipment; you need to be physically fit.

Are you prepared to be flexible with your time and calendar? If you want a 'nine to five' working day, then this is not the business for you. People hardly ever hire out a bouncy castle between the hours of 9 and 5 o'clock on a weekday. Most hires will be in the early evenings and at weekends. You will be leaving your old type of existence behind. At the same time, you will be in charge of your personal diary completely which is a benefit you will never want to lose.

I have no desire to put anyone off from following their dreams of running a profitable bouncy castle hire business but please take a moment to reflect on the points I have made in the above paragraphs. Not every person is suitable for this type of business.

Joining the BIHA

As a bouncy castle owner, I know full well that the business of hiring inflatables can be incredibly challenging and this industry can be lonely and at times the competition fierce.

What follows is an edited version of a promotional article that I wrote about the benefits of joining the BIHA and its associated social media forums where members exchange ideas and trade new and used equipment:

Our rewards and satisfaction can often be high in the non-monetary areas, but the joy can quickly disappear when all our energy is spent worrying about paying bills or making the mortgage payment.

So how do you balance the satisfaction of hiring inflatables with the hundreds of demands on you to start, run, and grow a successful hire business? You could be making mistakes that are costing you hundreds of pounds every month, without you even knowing it!

You probably already know that starting a bouncy castle hire business and turning a healthy profit is tough work, and growing it and making it successful is even more so. It is a demanding personal business to own and operate. The quickest route to long-lasting success as a bouncy castle owner is not about figuring it out for yourself. There is no need to struggle on your own. The BIHA is here to help you, and we will share our experiences with you.

This is a rare opportunity to discover the insider secrets and strategies of top bouncy castle/inflatable hire owners and operators who run very successful hire businesses.

Imagine a place where you can get personal advice from experienced professionals and experts, enjoy VIP access to a unique support system, plus get immediately useful resources in a private discussion forum and two Facebook groups from bouncy castle owners around the UK, (including some from overseas) - all of whom want you to succeed.

It is here! All the tools and resources you need. It does not matter if you are just starting out, or if you are a well-established owner with many years of experience. A membership at BouncyCastleOwner.com (This is the forum affiliated with the BIHA) will show you how to get more bookings, make more money, get more satisfaction and really enjoy the business of hiring bouncy castles and other play inflatables.

Whether you dream of starting your own inflatable hire business, or wonder how to best market and advertise your business, need to maintain staff loyalty, struggle with all the day-to-day dealings, or need help with the ever-changing demands of business ownership - The BIHA is here to support you, encourage, and guide you to make your dreams a reality.

Who Runs The BIHA Website, the two Facebook Groups and the Forum?

I run the BouncyCastleOwner.com website with help and advice from some very experienced and long-established members. I am nationally known as the founder of the BIHA, which has over 1,500 members. I had my own successful inflatable hire business from 1991 - 2005. I have also appeared live on GMTV and Channel 4 in 2008 to talk about the industry. More recently I have been interviewed by Sky TV and the BBC about safety aspects within the industry following some well-publicised incidents involving Inflatables and bouncy castles.

Having spoken to and emailed hundreds of aspiring, new, and long-time bouncy castle owners from around the UK, I have a unique insight into what some of the most successful business owners are doing correctly.

Just as importantly, I will outline the frequent mistakes that some of the new bouncy castle hire owners are making which is preventing them from being more successful.

You will learn from this insight. It is all real world, an applicable experience that you can take advantage of to make your inflatable hire business as successful as possible.

Now - I know what you are thinking…
"Can't I just go figure this out on my own for free?"
Can you? Probably!
Should you? It depends.

They say that 'time is money', and I believe it to be true. You can certainly click through the millions of pages online that include information on running a business, marketing, handling customer service issues, reading threads on free forums and spending countless hours trying to figure it out on your own.

This book plus membership of the BIHA will undoubtedly fast track your success. You can access 24/7, 365 days a year a specialised, comprehensive website resource for everything you need to start, run and grow your bouncy castle hire business.

BIHA and BouncyCastleOwner.com Members are NEVER Alone!

Hundreds of bouncy castle owners use the Facebook group to help grow their business every month. Revolutionary technology allows our team to work with members all over the UK, and even the whole world (wherever there is internet connection!) This website is relied on as an essential part of successful bouncy castle/play inflatable ownership. The information offered is both cutting-edge and has been tested over time.

We know what it takes to build a successful inflatable hire business. And we show you the best strategies to launch, expand, or take your bouncy castle business to the next level. With all the experience and knowledge you gain, you will have a major advantage to set yourself apart and stand out. BouncyCastleOwner is the definitive resource to get you there.

Shorten The Learning Curve to Success
We have created this resource to help bouncy castle owners so that you will not make costly mistakes or lose more time and energy on the areas of business that drain you and burn you out.

Just a fraction of our member resources could be worth a large amount of money for you and your business. The time and money savings are significant because you will be making the correct decisions about your business from day one. Some of our members report that they get a full return on their membership subscription within the first few days!
Are you beginning to see that this is an easy way to fast-track your success?

We have a created a place where you can save time and money with a minimal investment in your business. This unique learning environment is a place where each member can ask for advice and feedback and get it from other bouncy castle owners experiencing tangible success in their own businesses and who are willing to share how they are doing it.

Right! That is enough plugging of the BIHA for now. Let me summarise in a few paragraphs an overview of how to get started. Then I will expand each section with more detail in later chapters

How To Get Started
Research the Bouncy Castle businesses who operate in your geographical area.

The first thing to do is to look through all your local **newspapers**. Locate the classified section and then find the heading 'Entertainers' or 'Leisure'. Also look on **Google** to see if there is anyone else running a Bouncy Castle Hire Business. **Do not just look for one week**. Keep looking every week. If you do spot a regular advertiser, do not be put off. There is still room for you. When my first advertisement appeared, to my astonishment another one appeared that same week. But, as I found out later, it did not matter. The calls kept coming in; there seemed to be room for us all. In fact, I learned later that this new rival was actually giving my telephone number to any inquirers he could not supply himself.

This new local competition seemed to rely on just that one little advertisement every week. But it must have worked for him. Nobody keeps placing the same worded advertisement week in, week out - unless it is working well. Later on in this book, I will show you additional ways of generating enquiries that the competition probably will not have even thought of.

Once you have exhausted all the local papers and directories, go onto the internet and see who has a good website and from where they are running their business.

The internet is where most people look for a bouncy castle company today. As a matter of interest look at what device you are using to do these searches. Is it a computer or a laptop, a tablet or a mobile phone? Mobile internet is now the norm, and your customers will be looking for you on their phones. You need to be prepared and gear up for this. Online is the marketplace for new business leads. It is so different now compared to even ten years ago when Yellow pages book were heavy enough to be used as doorstops.

Be thorough and see who looks successful and has a current website. See who has old content and has no new events listed. It is usually quite obvious who the market leaders in your locality are.

Having found any likely competition, your next move is to pose as an interested customer. Telephone one of the advertisers. Ask questions like: "What is the cost per hire"? "Do you have insurance cover?" "What if it rains?" "Do I send a deposit?" Tell them you will telephone again when you have sorted out a date, but ask whether they have many days free! Look to see if they take online bookings.

Once you have gone through this procedure a couple of times, you will have a better idea of the 'going rate' and the booking methods of your rivals.

If you are lucky, there may be no rivals operating in your area. I have had many calls from people who lived about thirty miles away from my area. They have all explained how they have searched through all their local newspapers for weeks for a Bouncy Castle to hire. They, like me, found that the Yellow Pages did not help either.

I have hired out to a few customers in this situation, but have always pointed out that I have to charge them an extra £5 to £10 to cover the distance if they wanted delivery.

Just think, setting up a Bouncy Castle Hire Business if you live somewhere like this, you could virtually command the whole area.

I went to great lengths posing as a potential customer, to see how 'easy' it was to get hold of a party-size Bouncy Castle. I even telephoned toy shops and fancy dress hire stores. Even theatrical agents listed in my local Yellow Pages telephone directory.

They all told me what I wanted to hear - "Sorry, I don't know anyone who hires Bouncy Castles." I then looked under 'Entertainers'. There were plenty of magicians, puppet shows, balloon suppliers and caterers. But no Bouncy Castle Hirers.

By this time I knew that the local newspapers were the only place to find one. So you can see how I was convinced my Bouncy Castle Hire Business would work.

I am sure that you will be even more encouraged than I was at the time; if you find that your area has none at all. As mentioned earlier, this would be a golden opportunity to be the only Bouncy Castle Hire Business for miles.

Safecic.co.uk
One of the ramifications of increased concern for child protection is the need for you to consider registering with the Disclosure and Barring Service (DBS) This was formerly known as CRB (Criminal Records Bureau) checking for you and your staff. This sounds heavy and bothersome, but it is not an issue to ignore. More and more businesses are advertising that their staff are DBS compliant and customers see this as a

positive and sensible thing. Most schools and young peoples' group will require it as mandatory.

Safecic.co.uk provides guidance on child protection issues in line with current child protection legislation and promotes the Government's 'Every Child Matters' agenda. Established in 1999 Safecic.co.uk is a registered charity and is dedicated to promoting the welfare of all children and young people.

Safecic.co.uk Services is backed by a multi-agency team of very experienced and highly qualified child protection professionals; Safecic.co.uk provides a comprehensive range of services to help keep children safe.

At Safecic.co.uk they take a straightforward and practical approach and make tackling the subject easier through the use of guidance templates for writing child protection policies and risk assessments. They also offer distance-learning child protection training courses, DBS checks and up to the minute child protection information. In addition, Safecic.co.uk runs child protection seminars across the country for those wanting to explore the subject in more depth.

Through membership of Safecic.co.uk, you can access their self-audit tools thereby enabling you to carry out your own child protection risk assessment and tailor your own child protection policy from the Safecic.co.uk template. Where required, Safecic's child protection specialists will review and approve your risk assessment at no additional charge.

Safeguarding children, young people and vulnerable adults should be of paramount importance to everyone, not least because all organisations have a 'duty of care' towards all those who are involved in or who attend them. The Victoria Climbié and Bichard Enquiries graphically illustrate the overwhelming consequences for children and organisations when child abuse occurs. Specifically, they have caused a major shift in government policy to make the protection of children and young people everyone's business.

"Everyone working with children and families should be familiar with and follow their organisation's procedures and protocols for promoting and safeguarding the welfare of children in their area, and know who to contact in the organisation to express concerns about a child's welfare."

Safecic.co.uk has been working with a broad cross-section of voluntary groups and commercial organisations from a wide spectrum of sectors since 1999, including:

- Faith
- Uniformed Groups
- Arts/Theatre/Music
- Preschool/Play Groups
- General Youth Groups
- Museums/Libraries/Archives
- Village Halls/Community Centres
- Sports
- Education
- Government Agencies/Local Authorities
- Housing Associations
- Licensed Trades
- Retail
- Leisure activities
- Health

By joining the 2000 organisations already in membership, you will be able to access everything you need to safeguard children in your care.

The Safecic.co.uk team is drawn from an extensive range of over thirty professionals who are child protection experts within their own fields, e.g. police, social care services, education, youth offending, health, early years, victim support and advocacy.

Equipment needed to start up your business

Here is a list of what you are likely to need:

1. Bouncy Castle, inflation fan, anchor stakes, and sack trolley.

2. Heavy duty plastic sheeting 13 or 14 feet square for use as a shower cover. Builders' damp-proof membrane is ideal.

3. Electrical extension cable, 50-60 feet long.

4. Club hammer or mallet for knocking in anchor stakes

5. RCD circuit breaker (safety cut-out device for mains electric)

6. Robust plastic box for the storage of extension cable, anchor stakes, hammer, circuit breaker, instruction sheet, business cards or postcard advertisements.

7. Local map of your town and its surrounding area. You can use satellite navigation and online maps, but sometimes a simple paper map is the best option.

8. Desk diary for taking bookings, preferably two days to a page A5 size. You can also use your Google account if you have one for making appointments. In my experience, many people still keep a paper version of their diary. If the appointment makes it to the paper diary 'In Ink' then it is a firm booking. Anything else is a note or a possible booking.

9. Ledger book for recording takings etc., A4 size. (See the paperwork chapter for more on this)

10. Public Liability Insurance (for £1million of cover) Some local authorities will insist on £5million to £10 million public liability cover for inflatables to be put up on their land.

You may already own a circuit breaker, club hammer box, extension cable, diary, etc. if so, then there is not too much to obtain before you can get started. Some bouncy castles come with a shower cover as standard. I recouped the total cost of my equipment in only two months from starting up! There is a list of recommended manufacturers and suppliers on the BIHA website at biha.org.uk.

Finding Your First Bouncy Castle To Buy
To find your first castle can be daunting and intimidating. It is at this point that you are really making a commitment to your future and your business. The old method used to be looking through business opportunities papers and magazines in the hope of finding a manufacturer who was advertising their wares. You would think that it would have become easier in the 21st Century but for a number of reasons that is not the case.

When you search online to buy a bouncy castle the results are not very helpful. You get a mix of local bouncy castle hire companies and national manufacturers. The problem is that you have no idea who supplies trade bouncy castles and who supplies retail units that are unsuitable for the hiring business. All of the units that are advertised from local supermarkets and other retail chains are completely unsuitable for hiring out and is illegal under the Health and Safety at Work Act 1974 and also under PUWER Regulations 1998. It is also against 'best practice' see en14960. They would wear out very quickly and are not designed for heavy use.

You need to know that your investment is wise and sensible. You need good information about who manufactures quality inflatables and which company gives you good after-sales service. To that end, the BIHA has a list of recommended suppliers in the UK to help you make a start. See **www.biha.org.uk/about-the-biha/manufacturers/** Look at the BIHA Facebook group and ask questions about how to start up and what type of castle to buy for your first one. You will be amazed how helpful other business people are to a new company which is effectively setting up in competition. There is usually plenty of work out there.

Once you have done your research and decided who you are going to contact it is time to get on the phone and make some calls. Contact the Bouncy Castle companies that you find. See if any of them offer easy payment terms, or take credit cards. Many do.

Now, speaking from experience, initially do not buy anything over twelve feet square or it will not pack down small enough to transport it unless you have a large van. After all, that is the basis and the ease of the Bouncy Castle Hire Business. The smallest Bouncy Castle usually starts at about eight feet square, the next size up is normally around ten feet square, but this does vary between suppliers.

Check that an electrical inflation fan is included in the price. Decide whether you want a petrol driven fan or not. You will find that it is about £150 extra. This is handy for using at fetes or car boot sales held in the middle of a field for instance. But really, an electric fan should be adequate to start your business with.

Also, inquire if delivery and VAT are included on the price list or not. It varies between companies. If you are already self-employed and are registered for VAT, then you may be able to claim the VAT back. Check with an accountant. Some Bouncy Castle suppliers will even paint your chosen trading name and telephone number on your castle at no extra cost. Take advantage of this if they do, as it could mean even more bookings. Other people at the event can easily see and make a note of your telephone number. In fact, on my Bouncy Castles, I have avoided using a trade name altogether. I just had 'TO HIRE' followed by my telephone number. The reason for this was so that it would appear larger and more prominent.

Read the supplier's *'small print'* thoroughly. Check that there are no usage restrictions. Also, inquire as to whether a repair kit is included with your bouncy castle. Most bouncy castles come with a one year guarantee. With some suppliers, it is even a two-year guarantee.

Never buy 'TOY' Bouncy Castles to hire out
These castles are made of a nylon material and are inflated by a little blower which is not much bigger than a hair dryer! They tend to sag rather than bounce and are definitely not up to entertaining a horde of excited children! Typically they are being hired out slightly cheaper than proper castles even though they cost just a fraction as much to buy.

One final point is that they are manufactured to a different set of standards, the packaging would clearly state that they are not suitable for hire and if the operator was insured against public liability then the policy would be invalidated because the equipment is not suitable. Please be aware and choose who and where you buy your castle from carefully! Heavy Duty castles are the proper commercial type, they are regularly cleaned and maintained, and they pass annual safety inspections. Under the Health and Safety Work Act 1975, and PUWER (Provision and Use of Work Equipment Regulations 1998) toy inflatables cannot be legally hired out.

A Note About Buying Second Hand Bouncy Castles And Inflatables
I would never consider buying a second-hand inflatable or bouncy castle unless it is literally only a few weeks old. You must be sure that the castle you own is complete and in working order. Even then I would take great care in making a second-hand purchase.

If you come across a deal that sounds too good to be true, then believe the adage, *"If It Sounds Too Good To Be True Then It Probably Is!"* Ask yourself why the seller is selling the item and see if you find out why he/she is selling it. A second-hand unit could have a slow leak that is not noticeable when you see it demonstrated. There could be wear and tear on the seams or perhaps the fan has seen many hours of hard work and is on the way out.

With a new hire item, you have guarantees and security that you will never have when buying second hand.

By the way, if I was selling a second-hand bouncy castle, then I would give the prospective buyer the hiring history of it and clear it off at a bargain price with a clear 'buyer beware' note. A bit of honesty would solve all sorts of problems when selling second hand but not everyone is as honest as you or I might be.

If You Really Must Save Money and Buy Second Hand
Buying second-hand has always been a sensible alternative for many major purchases in life. Houses, cars, and boats, for example, are popular second-

hand purchases. Yet, buying second-hand also carries inherent risks. Are you getting a good deal or inheriting someone else's problems? You will need your eyes, your ears (and your nose!) and a little gut instinct to know if the second-hand inflatable you are looking at buying will be a good investment or a complete waste of money. Here are a few things to think about before you buy a second-hand inflatable.

Who is the manufacturer?
Is it a large manufacturer with a reputation to uphold or some chap on his own working out of a garage? The reputation and track record of the manufacturer can give you key information about the wisdom of your purchase.

Who is the seller?
Is the seller a private individual or the manufacturer? You may get a better price from a private individual, but a manufacturer is in a better position to repair an inflatable or offer a warranty.

A manufacturer also has his reputation to maintain. Let us face it; if you buy a used inflatable from a manufacturer and it turns out to be a great investment, you will probably return to him when you are ready to buy new! And also tell other hire companies and fellow BIHA members about him.

Why is the seller selling?
You may not get a straight answer to this one - but ask anyway. Some hire companies have a policy of never reselling inflatables. Fortunately, inflatables take up relatively little space and even hiring the inflatable a few times a year may deliver a better profit than the second-hand price would be.

If the answers you have received to this point are positive, it is time to have a look at the inflatable. The best way to evaluate an inflatable is, when it is inflated, and in person. If for some reason you cannot inspect it in person (for example you live a long distance from the seller), ask for a recent video of the inflatable in action.

Assuming you are able to inspect the unit in person, your eyes are the first tool to use in your evaluation. Look for obvious wear such as places where the thread is giving way, abrasions to the vinyl and spots where seams are starting to separate.

Examine the stress points. Turn it over and check the bottom. Does the unit appear to have been dragged repeatedly? Are there mould/mildew spots or tears? Are there spots with mismatched vinyl denoting an amateurish patching or repair job? Is it clean?

Types of inflatables to buy
One of the most enjoyable decisions, when you are starting in this business, is to decide what type of inflatables to invest it. The bouncy castles available from today's manufacturers are simply mind-blowing. I will now describe what type of inflatables are available and also the hire market that you should be aiming for.

The most popular size of bouncy castle is 12 feet x 15 feet

This type of standard size bouncy castle is the best to start off with because it will fit inside most customers' back gardens, and additionally, it will also fit inside most halls (which can be a lifeline in the winter) Also, this size of bouncy castle is not too heavy and can be handled by just one person. Back-garden parties will be your "bread and butter business" so this is why this size of castle is so popular. But a word of warning! You should automatically get lots of referrals every time your 12ft x 15ft castle goes out on hire, and you will quickly find that you need to buy a second castle, and then perhaps a third and fourth one etc. Try to be careful that you don't go overboard with investing in this type of castle, because come September, (unless there is an Indian summer) you will find that demand suddenly drops dramatically, as well as your income! Also, it's vitally important that you invest in a party theme that is suitable for both boys and girls. This will give you a bigger market.

Once you get experience of supplying castles to children's back garden parties, it will then give you vital experience as to whether or not you want to start expanding your business into more lucrative areas such as larger inflatables and the corporate and fundraising market etc.

Maintaining cash-flow in your new business is vitally important, and will help you to grow faster. Don't charge too little for your hires, you will probably want to take on staff at some point, and if your hire fee is too low, then you won't be able to pay your drivers, and as a result, your growth potential will be severely limited.

Adult Bouncy Castles
Once you get familiar with hiring bouncy castles to the children's market, then it's time for you to consider the adult hire market which can be much more lucrative due to higher rental fees. Examples include corporate events and fund-raising activities where the demand for bigger inflatables can be high.

But alongside this extra money comes the problem of unruly and drunk customers who are perhaps enjoying themselves a bit too much, and so the risk of damage to your inflatable increases. Also, collection times tend to be much later, so you have to factor that in when making a decision.

When you buy a bouncy castle (whether it's for children or adults) ensure that it is built to the European Standard en14960. Also, check with your manufacturer that they use high-grade PVC and that the bed is webbed (which will greatly extend its life). Also, check that the stress points are reinforced with additional stitching and further webbed. If you need a repair at the height of the season, it can be extremely frustrating and costly if it means that you are losing hires because you have to return the inflatable to the factory.

Slides & Combos
A bouncy castle slide combo is a bouncy castle with a slide attached to it (either front facing, or added to the side). These tend to be extremely popular because children love to both bounce and slide, and gives your customers more choice. They also command higher rental fees. Front

facing slides tend to be more popular with customers because they can keep an eye on the children more easily.

Inflatable slides on their own, are also a very popular hire product, and you will find that many of your customers will choose to hire both a bouncy castle and a slide. Do be aware though that once your slide goes beyond a certain height, then the insurance costs will increase quite dramatically. So, check with your insurance company first. Larger slides with a platform height of 10 feet or more should be targeted more to events where there will be a lot of children. In general slides of this height are not really suitable for the domestic market.

Obstacle Courses (Assault Courses)
Inflatable obstacle courses are an amazing hire product, are hugely popular and can earn you some serious money. However, try to resist the temptation of going too big initially because your "bread and butter" market will be domestic hires. Try to choose obstacle courses that are designed to take "add-ons" - that way; it can grow as your business grows! This is especially true when you start to get corporate enquiries. Once you get corporate clients - you may want to invest in larger obstacle courses.

Other inflatables include Disco Domes, Ball-Ponds, Interactive Inflatables, Inflatable Games, Rodeo Bulls, Surf Simulators, Gladiator Duel, Whack a Mole, and Pole Joust.

Some final thoughts
If possible always ask for proof of purchase for two reasons. One is to know the true age of the inflatable. The other is to know the unit is not stolen.

Consider more than just price when buying used. Take into consideration the amount of repair work required before buying for price only. Sometimes it is better to spend a little more money and be safe than sorry. Always ask for test certificates, manuals and any maintenance records.

With regards to buying a second-hand blower/fan. Have a good look at the electrical connections, and check for wear, cracks and tears. Preferably the unit will have been recently PAT tested. Ensure you hear the blower working. If it rattles, then this may be due to worn bearings or a loose nut on the impeller. Check the blades of the impeller, are they in good condition?

When looking at second-hand inflatables and blowers, it is always a very good idea to take someone with you who is experienced and knows what to look out for.

Safety Testing For Bouncy Castles
For several years now there has been a national scheme to improve safety in inflatable play, and it is fast becoming adopted as the means by which end users can purchase or hire a bouncy castle or another inflatable in the knowledge that it has been tested, inspected and passed by a qualified independent third party.

Prior to PIPA (Pertexa Inflatable Play Accreditation - www.pipa.org.uk) bouncy castles and other play inflatables were already subjected to health and safety legislation. However, enforcement and monitoring was a problem for authorities because standards varied so much throughout the industry. However, that has all changed now since the HSE asked the industry to devise an inspection scheme to meet their strict criteria. After much consultation, the industry trade bodies, BIHA (British Inflatable Hirers Alliance), IPMA (Inflatable Play Manufacturers Association) and RPII (Register of Play Inspectors International) and the HSE have set up and adopted the PIPA scheme as 'best practice' for the industry.

Here are the latest PIPA guidelines for people who want to hire a bouncy castle for their event. It makes useful reading from our point of view in the industry.

The inflatable play is normally a very safe and pleasurable way for children to exercise whilst having fun. The PIPA scheme ensures that equipment is tested to a recognised standard both before first use and annually thereafter.

ALWAYS

- Have regard to the equipment's intended use
- Bear in mind that users who are outside the intended weight or height range can injure themselves and other users
- Make sure the blower is at least 1.2 metres from the inflatable
- Remember that a serious injury can occur if a user strikes the blower unit
- Make sure the equipment has a current test certificate
- Look for the PIPA tag and check its validity on this site
- Use surround mats if provided as these negate identified risks
- Ensure that children are supervised at all times by a responsible adult. The vast majority of accidents occur through a lack of or poor supervision
- Anchor the inflatable to the ground and ensure that you use every anchor point. Even in non-windy conditions the inflatable can move and creep (perhaps taking it dangerously too close to the blower)
- Hire your inflatable from a reputable operator. Some will try to cut costs on safety by not using the PIPA scheme - always check
- Follow the instructions given to you by the hirer - these are there for the safety of your children
- Hire on the basis of the safest - not the cheapest
- Deflate the inflatable after its use to prevent unsupervised use

NEVER

- Allow users to climb on to the walls - most accidents happen this way!
- Deflate the inflatable whilst it is in use as the users can strike the ground heavily if you do
- Use the inflatable if you have any doubt as to its safety

- Throw objects or other people on to the inflatable
- Allow users onto the inflatable in high winds

Promotional Items

Now, this is important. The worst thing you can do is not take advantage of your very first hiring. For example - a parent has just hired your bouncy castle for their son's birthday party. You have just pocketed your first £80 or so. Well, so far, so good. But remember, at the party, there may also be the parents of the other children. Their children all have birthdays too. So you need to push your name and telephone number as much as possible. This can be done in a number of ways.

Here is a list of items that will help you achieve this:-

- Postcard size (88 x 142mm) 'advertisements' of your service (leave a bundle in your storage box).
- Leaflets. A5 in size (210 x148mm) which can also double as mini-posters.
- Business cards with your address and telephone number. Or just your telephone number alone.
- Envelopes.
- Receipt book and rubber stamp. Or better still, printed pads, with duplicate sheets.
- Letter headings -- size A5 (210 X 148mm), or A4 (297 X 210mm).
- First class postage stamps.
- Roller Banners

Later on, in this chapter, I will show you how you can organise and order your printing in a most cost-effective way. I will also show you all the shortcuts and money-saving tips I have learnt.

Special Tip -if you are on your first hire, or even your first 10 hires you should hang around and see how people use your bouncy castle and also talk to party guests about your hire service. Wear a shirt or top with your company logo on and just chat to people about your business. You will almost certainly obtain some good leads by being present in this way.

Whom Do You Hire To?
The beauty of the bouncy castle Hire Business is the almost endless range of possible customers. You will find that the home birthday party will be your biggest customer attraction. Let us face it, wherever you live there are families with children, and they all have birthdays! However, most of your bookings will be for weekends. Whilst a child's birthday may be on a weekday, the party will probably be organised on the Saturday or Sunday.

Other regular customers are schools. I have hired out many times to school fetes. They charge the children about £1 for five minutes 'bouncing'. With a twelve-foot square castle taking about eight children at a time and the fete usually lasting about three hours, it is possible for them to take about £200, less the hire charges of say, £65, they could make about £135 profit. Of course, you might have to be present to monitor the public use of your castle, and this has to be factored in. Some schools will be organised with teachers designated to monitor the children on the bouncy castle. Others will not. This detail is worth agreeing before the hire takes place.

Another possibility is pubs. More and more pubs are trying to encourage families to their premises. Therefore a beer garden with a bouncy castle could be just what the publican needs to help attract custom. Parents could enjoy a drink while the children are amused bouncing on the castle. If you contact some pub landlords well in advance of the summer, they will be able to mention your bouncy castle to their regulars and other customers and mention it in their local newspaper advertising in good time. Charge about £120 - £250 for a whole weekend. This depends to some degree on what you are hiring out. (Please note that some insurance companies will not provide public liability insurance for licensed premises, so please check the small print on your insurance documents or telephone them).

Next - car dealers. Let us say a local dealer has a new model launch at the showroom. You can offer to hire them your bouncy castle for the corner of their showroom. Parents can view the new car while the children are kept amused at the same time. You could probably work out a special weekend price-deal with the owner. £120 - £200 is not an uncommon figure. Watch the national press for new car launches by the manufacturers. Then you have got time to inform your local garage about your offer before they plan their showroom launch. That way, again, they have plenty of time to include a mention of a bouncy castle in their promotional literature and newspaper advertising.

Builders - By this, I mean builders of housing estates, family homes, etc. you could supply your bouncy castle at the site next to the show house. Parents could safely leave their children playing on the Castle while they view the show house in peace. Keep an eye on Estate Agents promoting new housing developments. Contact them as early on as possible.

Cricket and other sports clubs might like to hire your Bouncy Castle for children of parents watching a game on a weekend afternoon. I hired one of mine out every August Bank Holiday for the local cricket club's charity match.

Approach the manager of your local DIY Superstore. They have normally got the space for a bouncy castle, and may perhaps like to link the hire with an open day or a promotional drive of some kind. Again, a weekend hire charge of £120 - £200 is a good guide.

Here is a list of other possible customer outlets who would all have an interest in hiring:

- Car Boot sales/events
- Shopping Precincts
- Village Halls
- Supermarkets
- Rugby Clubs
- Zoos
- Football Clubs
- Barbecues
- Cub and Scout Groups
- Hockey Clubs
- Brownie/Guide Groups
- Golf Clubs
- Shop Openings
- Beach Parties/Barbecues
- Garden Centres; Mother and Toddler Clubs

- Tennis Clubs
- Christening Parties
- Wedding Receptions
- Playgroups.

Safety
Obviously, with children, safety is paramount. Thankfully, a bouncy castle is one of the safest things on which children can play. Nevertheless, it is strongly recommended that you supply your hirers with an RCD Circuit Breaker, as mentioned earlier in the section on electrical equipment. This device will cut the power immediately should, for any reason, the electrical cable be cut, or any exposed electrical connections get wet. When you purchase your fifty or sixty-foot extension cable, make sure you buy one with rubber plugs and sockets. Some Circuit Breakers are also available combined with a plug as one unit. A good way of ensuring it is used and also returned to you!

The anchor stakes normally supplied with most bouncy castles should be well hammered into the ground. An adult should be present at all times when the Castle is in use. Emphasize these points in your instruction sheet which you supply to each customer (Instruction sheet template details later on in the book).

Indoors, say in a local hall, the castle is usually more stable. If your castle has anchor straps attached to the base sections, then these could be weighted down with sandbags.

Finally, do not forget to arrange Public Liability Insurance.

Heath & Safety
Health and safety is extremely important and when you pay attention to it, then it will help your hire business to flourish and grow. Never cut corners. Every time you put out an inflatable for hire, it is vital that you give your customers various documents such as Terms and Conditions of Hire. Some customers will also ask for a Risk Assessment or even a Method Statement. Some customers will ask for proof of your insurance and even copies of your test certificates on your inflatables, and PAT testing certificates, etc.

You will want to demonstrate high levels of safety to your customers and potential customers.

Below is a list of the fundamentals of safe inflatable hire. Please also try to buy a copy of BS EN 14960:2013. Also, bear in mind that the Health and safety at Work Act 1974 stipulates that you owe a duty of care to users on any equipment which is hired out.
This is the LAW!

This by all means is not an extensive list and your duty of care should go above and beyond this level.

Public Liability Insurance
Rather bizarrely, this is not a compulsory requirement but I would strongly advise that you buy public liability insurance. In today's compensation culture, you will want to make sure your business and your personal assets are covered in case you are negligent and a claim is made against you.

The recommended public liability insurance cover is £5 million pounds. This figure will be asked for by many schools, universities and councils etc when supplying them inflatables. Some councils insist on £10 million pounds of cover.

At the back of this book, you will see a list of companies which provide PL insurance cover.

Inflatable Testing
This part is compulsory within the inflatable hire industry but is often not done by many bouncy castle hire companies. When hiring inflatable equipment you become subject to the health & safety at work act 1974. This places onus on the hirer and it's employees and the manager/owner of anywhere the equipment will be used to ensure the equipment is safe to use at all times.

Provision and Use of Play Equipment Regulations (PUWER) requires that all work equipment, including inflatable play, must be tested by a "competent person" on a regular basis. Inspection by a "competent person" prior to first use and annually thereafter satisfies the provision that the equipment is suitable and safe for its intended use.

In order to comply with this provision there are a number of certification schemes you can use. These are PIPA, RPII and thirdly ADIPS. The recommended scheme is PIPA which uses an online database and once under the PIPA scheme all details for the inflatable can be brought up online.

It is important to mention that these three schemes only apply to inflatables where users are bouncing or sliding on line.

Method Statements & Risk Assessing
Managing the health and safety of any business must control the risks in the workplace. Risks are assessed by thinking about what might cause harm to people and decide whether reasonable steps are taken to prevent harm. This is known as a risk assessment and it is something that is required by law to be carried out.

A visual risk assessment is suffice for a small garden hire and no paperwork is needed, although I would advise to get a good disclaimer form signed by the hirer at every hire. Large events I recommend a check list which is signed by yourself and any event organiser on the day of the event.

Method statements are not lawfully required to be carried out. However, I recommend method statements to ensure all your employees have a good knowledge and understanding of safe set up and supervision of all your inflatable equipment.

Demonstrating good inflatable hire practices
Keeping everyone safe when using your inflatable hire equipment should be paramount on your list. There are a number of safety procedures you

can implement into your bouncy castle hire business to achieve a high level of safety.

The following points are a guide only and not an extensive list of safety procedures. I recommend buying a copy of bs en 14960. You are then armed with all the knowledge you need to keep everyone safe when using your inflatable hire equipment.

1) Make sure any inflatable you purchase has been built to the bs en 14960 standard. All reputable inflatable manufacturers will use this standard when building their inflatables.

2) Make sure your inflatables are anchored correctly. Most inflatable products will be used on a grassed surface using steel anchors at 380 mm length and a diameter of 16 mm.

If you are using the inflatable on a hard surface outdoors a ballast of 163 kg should be used on each anchor point. This can be achieved this on inflatables outdoors by drilling and bolting to any solid surface. Block paving and slabs are not suitable for this method, solid surfaces such as concrete or tarmac are needed.

3) Visually check the inflatable before every use and make sure it is fit for its intended purpose. Check all electrical equipment and make sure the blower is tested at regular intervals to prevent electric shock. All electrical equipment should be PAT tested.

4) Always supply the customer with operation instructions and safety procedures in the event of failure. Many accidents happen whilst in the care of the hirer and simple safety practices could avoid many injuries sustained by this type of negligence.

BIHA and TIPE
Both organisations offer crucial advice for new and experienced inflatable hire companies. The BIHA promotes safe and responsible use of inflatable equipment. The BIHA also runs a Facebook group, where hirers can network and support each other.

TIPE also promotes high standards of professionalism, responsibility and safety ethics within the inflatable play industry and offers a service to its subscribers to assist in running a safer and better inflatable hire business.

Presenting a Professional Image
It is important from the beginning to try to portray a professional image to your new part-time business. Obviously, you will want to keep your initial expenses at the outset to a minimum. But cutting your costs too far may produce an amateurish image.

You have probably received leaflets and sales letters that have an unprofessional appearance. Badly spelt and printed; in fact, many are just faded photocopies, hurriedly put together.

How do you start to present a professional image? The first thing is to create a logo. Now, I do not mean a symbol; I mean a name you can trade under, typeset in a particular style that you can use wherever you want your name to appear. A very distinctive typeface could be your logo. It will need to be bold and, bearing in mind that bouncy castles should represent fun for children, also easily readable by adults. After all, they will be the ones making that initial inquiry and eventually paying you.

Of course, you do not have to use a trade name if you do not want to. I decided to call my business just 'ALL STARS LEISURE'. The reason for this was that I wanted to try to attract customers as quickly as possible.

An advantage of having an obvious name like this is that the internet search engines like business names with good search terms. So if you were looking to hire a bouncy castle then what would you type into a search engine? My guess would be something like *'Bouncy Castle'* or *'Bouncy Castle Hire'*. In both these cases, my business name would feature highly in the search engines result.

Once you have decided on a trading name, you will need to design your logo style. Now you can have a go yourself, or, as I did, get a professional graphic designer to give you two or three rough ideas. Many Instant-Print shops offer a design and artwork service as well as just printing.

If your local instant-print shop does not offer this service, look online. You should find a good selection of companies and 'one-man-band' freelancers. If you can, try and pick a freelancer. The chances are they will be cheaper than a design studio.

Sketch out any ideas you have, together with a possible typeface you like. Clip typeface samples that appeal to you from magazines, or newspapers. This will help to convey what sort of 'feel' you would like to aim for. Do not forget to get a quote before any work is commenced.
I started by giving a local freelance graphic a rough sketch:

I told him I wanted a 'loose' style of typeface. Big and bold enough to stand out and be almost read at a glance. The design was then worked up to a finished stage, known as 'artwork'. This was then given to me, which I, in turn, gave my printer who made up my stationery needs ready for printing.

For example, they printed 6,000 leaflets, black on yellow paper, trimmed to A5 size, for £70 . The local instant-print shop wanted £85, and I would have to pay when I collected my leaflets! These are old prices from when I started my business, but you will be amazed at how the prices come down if you order in bulk.

I suggest that you approach about three or four small local printers and get quotes based on the tips mentioned in the section 'Leaflets/Posters' and compare them.

Call each printer in person. It is better to find one who is able to give you helpful hints and the benefit of his experience, rather than just low prices. Reliable and accurate 'completion dates' are important, especially when tying-in with pre-determined launch advertisements.

Now based on my experience, below is listed what you will need in the way of stationery and promotional literature (note: sizes are mentioned in millimetres as printers prefer to work in metric).

Postcard Size Advertisement (88 x 142mm)
These can be placed in newsagents and sub-post office window display boards in your local area. They can also be used as giveaways to customers. Store some in your plastic storage box of accessories. That way they are at every customer's venue and can also be given away to possible future customers.

I even managed to encourage some of my customers to insert a postcard into each of the children's party bags that they took home with them, thereby reaching the parents who were not even at the parties. If hiring to pubs, ask the landlord if he would place some cards on his bar. Keep your cards in a small plastic bag with a rubber band around, so they stay clean.

You may find that 500 business cards will last you a year or two. But the postcards may only last you one year as these will be used the most as giveaways at parties, etc. so the following year will probably mean you only need to reprint the postcards. Ask for them to be set 4 per page so for example; you get 400 for the price of printing 100.

Leaflets/Posters
Try to convey the 'fun' image of bouncy castles. Get your designer or printer to add balloons or clowns somewhere. Do not forget to keep using your logo. As for size, A5 (210 x 148mm) is the most economical for leaflets or mini posters.

Two A5's side by side on the long edge make exactly A4. So get your printer or graphic designer to make up your artwork for two leaflets side by side. They will probably suggest this anyway. Obtain a quote for printing about 3,000 A4. Once cut down the centre, you will now have 6,000 A5 - for the price of printing 3,000.

Print black on yellow paper for maximum impact. Use as leaflets for the launch of your business. Any spares can be used as handouts or posters at a later date.

Receipt Pads
You could purchase a pre-printed receipt pad from your local stationers. But having come this far with your own logo, it makes sense to see the professional image right through. Again A5 (210 x148mm) is the ideal size. If your designer or printer lays out the artwork as shown below, you can print on A4 and trim through the middle giving you an A5 printed receipt sheet and a ready-made blank for your carbon copy. Get them made up into pads of ten or twenty leaves and use carbon paper.

Note: Make sure that you add a small asterisk (*) next to the section where you write in the deposit amount. Then add (in small type) at the base of the receipt 'non-returnable'. This should cover you for anyone cancelling at the last minute after you have possibly turned away other possible customers.

You can use an online invoicing system which will save you time when you begin to get busy but to start with a simple paper receipt system will be perfectly adequate.

Stickers
These are not a necessity, but I will include them here in case you want to use them at a later stage.

Obtain some A4 sized 'crack back' self-adhesive label sheets from your printer or stationery. Many are pre-cut and ready to print onto. If you have access to a photocopier, you could save money by copying your logo artwork directly onto the stickers by feeding them straight into the photocopier. Peel off a couple and stick to the sides of your inflation fan, and your accessory box. In fact, anywhere where your logo could be seen whilst on hire.

Instruction Sheet
Some bouncy castle manufacturers supply an instruction leaflet on how to erect the bouncy castle, but this will often carry their logo and address. Keep your image going by having it neatly re-typed onto an A4 size sheet of paper headed with your logo and telephone number.
If they do not supply an instruction sheet, erect the castle yourself and make notes on the procedure. Then later, write out your own instructions. Keep it concise and straight to the point.

Once you have checked and double-checked your instructions, and had them typed, you could then photocopy twenty or thirty and keep them handy. Replace the one or two supplied in your accessory box each time they come back dog-eared or torn. I found a better way was to create one good quality instruction sheet and then have it encapsulated in plastic. This makes it strong and robust as well as waterproof. A photographic studio or an instant-print shop will probably have a laminating machine. It should only cost one or two pounds.

Launching Your Business
After taking delivery of your bouncy castle, you need to set a launch day. This will be the day you start trading. The day your first advertisement appears. The day you distribute your leaflets. The day you listen in earnest for the telephone to ring.

When to Launch
Late March or early April is about the right time to start. It will be the Easter Holidays, and then with summer approaching with school holidays, it is the ideal time to begin. You will probably find a slight increase in bookings around that time. Having said this if you are ready to start now, then just get on with it. There is no magic to this. Hard work and consistent promotion will help you get started at any time of the year.

So where do you start? Well, the first thing to do is to get those A5 leaflets printed. The best way to launch your bouncy castle hire business is to try and cover as many angles as possible. Remember, your ideal target customers are the parents of three to ten-year-olds who live in a house with a reasonably sized garden in your local town.

To reach that sort of customer, you could take out a large advertisement in your local newspaper. In my opinion, though this is a false economy. The newspaper will probably be thrown away after a couple of days. Plus, not everybody buys the local paper. That is kept until a later date. Hardly anybody will bother to cut out your small advertisement and keep it. A distinctive, coloured paper leaflet can be an eye-catching advantage.

Place your postcards the same week in your local newsagents' windows. In towns, newsagents tend to charge around £2.00 per week. Local surrounding village stores or newsagents often only charge 50p or 70p per week.

Now here is something interesting - and surprising. I live in a town surrounded by small villages. When I launched my bouncy castle Hire business, I put postcards in all the town's newsagents and all the sub-post office windows, with about seven or eight around the different village newsagents and general stores. Well, four months later I was amazed. I pulled about six to eight enquiries from the village placed postcards, and absolutely none from the busy high street placed postcards! It may work differently where you live, but it is worth bearing in mind when choosing the placing of postcards. Especially as regards to cost, etc.

I found that over the next six months, enquiries from my leaflets were still coming in. proving what I had mentioned earlier. People were saving them until they needed to book nearer the time of their child's birthday.

Why do businesses use leaflets posted through letterboxes?

What do you do when you get a bundle of leaflets through your door? Do you keep them or throw them away? Do you get annoyed with all the harm to the environment? Do you put up a sign saying 'No Free Papers' on your front door? Well, whatever you do let me tell you that leaflets work! If you produce leaflets and get them through enough letterboxes, you will have a stream of new customers to your hire business.

I have a friend who was made redundant and decided to go into business for himself. (not bouncy castle hire, but the example is relevant as his business was in peoples' homes) He did some training at his local Adult Learning Centre and some industry-specific training for the products and service he was planning. Then came the day to launch.

They had no customers and no track record. They arranged for 10,000 leaflets to be printed in black and white (They could not afford colour) and my friend started walking around some housing estates delivering leaflets. In the first week, he personally delivered 6,000 leaflets and was completely exhausted. His wife was a stay at home mum with two small children and took calls for £3,000 worth of business while her husband was delivering the leaflets. In 1990 that was a lot of money.

That business ended up employing eleven people and leasing two local business units until he retired in 2013. The point of the story is to say that leaflets delivered through doors work - whether you like it or not.

How To Track Enquiries
Keep a sheet of paper handy next to your telephone or in the back of your bookings desk diary. Head it up something like this:

Just tick a box when you have deduced from your caller how they came by your telephone number. Over a period of two to three months, you will see a pattern emerging of the best media to continue with and, consequently, what media to drop and not bother with.

Here is a method I used to save asking each caller, "Where did you see my advertisement?" In my leaflet, I mentioned the size of the bouncy castle, the hire charge plus accessories. In my newspaper advertisements, I did not mention size or price. So when a caller asks the hire charge, then you know it is a newspaper response. If they just want to know a certain date, it usually means it is a leaflet or postcard response.

I know someone else who asks, *"Were you recommended to us?"* which always gave them the information about where the lead had come from. When they find out it is a recommendation they go out of their way to thank the recommender.

Ideas for inflatables for older children and adults at private parties and events

There are different types of inflatables that you can invest in that will be popular for private parties and events (especially corporate events). With numerous suppliers offering a wide range of activities, there is sure to be something to suit everyone, providing a hilarious spectacle for contestants and spectators alike.

Sumo Wrestling
The revered Japanese art of Sumo has become increasingly popular. Along with inflatable sumo suits for the participants, protective headgear and neck braces are supplied for the sake of safety. Two oversize wrestlers try to shove each other out of the circular ring on the supplied Sumo mat.

Kangaroo Boxing
This is another increasingly popular competitive activity. The supplied inflatable boxers' outfits include a padded suit, kangaroo-shaped head protector (with built-in Aussie style hat), huge kangaroo feet and oversize boxing gloves. As with Sumo, combatants strive to battle each other out of the ring marked on a padded mat.

Gladiator Duel and Pole Joust
Based on the TV show, **Gladiator**, Duel provides a great test of balance and dexterity as contenders attempt to knock their adversary from a podium using an inflatable, padded 'pugil stick'. Suitable for outdoor and indoor use, and requires a space of 25` square with 12` height clearance. A similar, balance-challenging activity is the Inflatable Pole Joust, in which competitors armed with a padded pugil stick attempt to dislodge their opponent from a padded wooden pole, onto the soft inflatable bed beneath.

Bungee Run
Bungee Run is a brilliant two-player bungee game ideal for events as strategy is more important than brute strength. Each competitor starts from the middle of an inflatable and must place 3 batons on the posts of a matching colour at opposite ends of the inflatable bungee run. The players

are attached to the same bungee rope, which will only stretch so far until one is unceremoniously bungee'ed backwards!

Rodeo Bull Ride
The popular Rodeo Bull ride is an entertaining, amusing centrepiece for any event. Such rides are generally controlled by a trained operator, and the ride is surrounded by a soft inflatable for a safe landing when the rider is predictably unseated. Some rides are computerised, with riding times shown on a large, LCD display for the benefit of spectators. Ideal for use indoors or out, with an inflatable marquee often provided in case of inclement weather.

Bucking Sheep Ride
The Bucking Sheep is a hilarious slant on the above-mentioned Rodeo Bull and will have both riders and onlookers laughing aloud. Some suppliers offer the Rodeo Bull and Bucking Sheep as part of the same event package, and they can be interchanged in a few minutes by a trained operator.

The right choice of an inflatable-based activity can greatly enhance the enjoyment of any private party or event.

How To Start Up The Right Way From Day One Running Your Business Part Time
By far the safest way to start up your new business is to do it part-time. If you have a job, then you have the income to live off while you establish your new Bouncy Castle Business. Even if you hate your current job and cannot wait to stop, you should be very careful about this and not hand your notice in until your income from your new bouncy castle business is well established.

You will probably be running your new business on the weekends as this is when most hires take place. So you can plan around this assuming your current employment is mostly on Monday to Fridays. You will be working seven days a week and dashing around like a madman, but you will get the rewards if you persist. Losing the income from your work will hinder the expansion and success of your business.

If you have lost your job and your new Bouncy Castle business is what you plan to do I would still try and find an income source to help tide you over while you get started. I know you will not want to follow that advice, but I have to be honest, I have seen too many business people set up and make a great start to their hire business only to fail simply because it was underfunded.

I once presented a business plan to a high flying business executive. I had all the sales and profit projections set out neatly for the next three years. I had estimated the costs and felt convinced I was on to a winner. The executive looked at my plan for a few minutes and then looked at me in the eye. He said that I should redo the business plan but halve the sales and double the costs. If it still worked, then he would consider helping me. I was shocked that he said this at the time, but years later I am completely grateful to this wise man. He stopped me in my tracks with one sentence that saved me from a huge business failure. What I found, of course, was that I had not allowed for any contingency or unexpected costs in the plan. With the new sales and costs calculated the business plan did not work. Not even close!

If you have been made redundant and have a nice pot of money to start your business, then I would still be careful and not invest the whole amount in your planned business. You will still need something to live off while you establish your new business.

Taking The Leap Into Full Time
"How long should I stay part time before I go full time?" I get asked this question a great deal, and there is no quick answer. But here are some thoughts that might help you make the correct decision.

You will almost certainly want to go full time and choosing the right moment can be difficult. But staying part-time will also provide you with a lot of problems as it starts to become a success. You will start getting lots of castle hires and find that you have no spare time for a real life away from work. Your customers might realise that you are under a lot of pressure and see that you are not providing the best service for them.

Not only that. Your health will suffer if you do not control your schedule. Working full time, while running a part-time business, requires exemplary time management skills and a lot of self-control. You can only maintain it for so long.

Here are some of the deciding factors to help you make this all-important decision.

How Is It Going?
Are you hiring out bouncy castles three or four times a week with a full set of bookings for the coming months? Are you getting referrals from your existing customers? Is your bank account looking healthier than it has for years? Is there potential for you to increase your sales immediately if you went full time?

Take a good look at your part-time business and discuss it with your partner or a business friend who you can trust. Be honest with yourself and try not to dream too much. Is your part-time business really taking off so that it will suffer if you do not go full time?

Are You In Profit?
More than that, do you have money in your bank account that is free to use for your business and for your living expenses? You need to be sure that you can exist and live without your regular income from your full-time job while you transition to going into business full time. It is a season of change that will put you and your finances under pressure.

If you have been helped by family or friends with loans and other assistance, then you need to consider paying back everything you owe. Love only goes so far. You still need to pay back the people who have helped you get started.

Family Considerations
Talk about this with your close family. They need to be with you in the decision. Even if they think you are a bit crazy to give up your job; still try to get them on board with some level of assent and agreement. If you go

off on your own making life and financial decisions that affect them without full consultation, then you are at best being selfish and inconsiderate.

One thing you can agree is your hours. When you are planning to work and when you are going to take time off. I always book at least one day off work completely. If I do not do this, then my business would take over my life completely.

What Is In It For You?
Think about why you are doing this business and what you get out of it. Consider whether you can really keep going without a boss making demands of you and your time. Are you a self-starter type of person who has the confidence and gumption to run their own life even when times get tough?

Make sure that you will earn enough money to enjoy your life. Remember that some months you will have plenty of income from your business. But there will be other times when you are strapped for cash and need to rein things in for a short while. Can you live like that and enjoy it?

How To Make Sure You Are In Profit From Day One
In any bouncy castle hire business (especially if you have corporate clients), cash flow -money coming in and money going out -is absolutely vital to the continuation and success of your business. Money going out is the simple part, there are always expenses such as advertising, diesel, rent, supplies, replacing equipment, salaries, etc., that you need to pay. But sometimes, getting paid by your customers -particularly if they are large corporate clients, can be a slow and time-consuming process. Here are some essential tips to help you bring that money in.

Customers may be slow to pay, which will adversely affect your business's cash flow. It could mean that you might have to dig into your cash reserves to pay your bills. It may also mean that you have to spend time as a bill collector making phone calls or perhaps even sending out statements and collection notices to remind customers of past due bills.

How do you get your customers to pay on time?

Start by always having a signed contract or proposal. Although this seems obvious, it is important to discuss payment terms in the contract, with approval by both parties. Make sure that your contract includes not only when payment is due, but what the penalties are for late payment.

Include all relevant information on your invoices. Invoices should include more than just your client's name and services provided. Include when payment is due, late payment penalties and a contact name and phone number for any questions about the invoice.

Do you provide inflatable hire services to government bodies or large corporations? Government bodies and large corporations generally have cut-off dates for each invoice payment cycle. You may have to get your invoice in before a certain date, or they will not pay it until the next payment cycle. For example, you may have to have your invoice in by the 25th of the month, or it may sit in someone's inbox for another month. Ask the accounts payable department when they need your invoice, so you receive payment on time.

Send out your invoices promptly. You may do everything for your bouncy castle rental business from marketing to meeting with potential clients. It is easy to put some things off, but do not let your invoices be one of them. Make sure to send out your bills at the same time each month, or if your contract indicates that you bill right after service is completed, then send out the invoice immediately.

Many bouncy castle companies require bills to be paid within 30 days. Perhaps you could offer discounts if the customer pays their invoice early. Consider offering a 2% -3% discount if they pay the invoice within 10 days. Many of your clients will take advantage of the discount.

To ensure the cash keeps flowing in sooner, consider shortening your billing cycles. Instead of having a payment due in 30 days, require payment in 15 days. To avoid any confusion state the specific due date on your invoices.

Ask for payment up-front. Although this is not a typical payment method for corporate clients to pay a hire business, for many other businesses getting payment up-front is standard. Offer an incentive for your corporate customers to pay up-front -discounts, preferred delivery/collection times, or free add-ons, etc.

When signing up a new corporate customer, ask if they have special billing needs. As with government entities, other corporate customers may have specific deadlines to process invoices. You may have corporate clients who prefer to be billed mid-month and not the end or first of each month.

Give your clients an alternative of paying by credit card. If you do not accept credit cards, think of setting up an account on the Internet (through PayPal or similar payment system). These companies allow you to invoice your clients through e-mail and then they can use their credit card to pay for your services.

Check with your clients regularly to make sure they are satisfied with the inflatable hire services your company is providing. Clients have been known to withhold payment if they are not happy with their service even though they have not told you there is a problem!

Remember, your clients are in business to make a profit, and so are you. Getting paid is how you pay your employees, grow your business and pay your bills. Make sure that your payment policies are stated ahead of time, communicate with your clients and provide a good service. Keeping a good incoming cash flow is vital to the stability and growth of your business. Do not be afraid to let your customers know that you expect prompt payment for a job well done!

Keeping Running Costs Under Control

In order to maintain good cash flow, while running a bouncy castle hire business, it is vital that you reduce your business costs as much as possible, especially in these times of economic uncertainty.

Here are ten ideas for reducing your costs in your business.

1. Free Stuff

You should try visiting some of the thousands of freebie sites on the internet before buying your business supplies. You can find free stationery, business cards, software, graphics, online business services, etc.

2. Barter

If you have a business, you could be bartering for goods and services with other businesses. You should try to trade for something before you buy it. Barter deals usually require little or no money.

3. Network

Try networking your business with other businesses. This will cut down on your marketing and advertising costs. You may also try bartering goods and services with them.

4. Wholesale/Bulk

You will save money buying your business supplies in bulk quantities. You could get a membership at a wholesale warehouse or buy them through a mail-order wholesaler. Buy the supplies you are always running out of.

5. Borrow/Rent

Have you ever purchased business equipment you only needed for a small period of time? You could have just borrowed the equipment from someone else or rented the equipment from a General Hire store.

6. Online/Offline Auctions

Generally speaking, you can find lower prices on business supplies and equipment at online and offline auctions. I am not saying all the time, but before you go pay retail for these items try bidding on them first.

7. Plan Ahead

Make a list of business supplies or equipment you will need in the future. Keep an eye out for stores that have big sales. Purchase the supplies when they go on sale before you need them.

8. Used Stuff

If your business equipment and supplies do not need to be new, buy them used. You can find used items at used stores, yard sales, and here in the UK, the ever popular car-boot sales. Used stuff for sale message boards and newsgroups, etc.

9. Negotiate

You should always try to negotiate a lower price for any business equipment or supplies. It does not hurt to try.

10. Search

You can always be searching for new suppliers for your business supplies and equipment. Look for suppliers with lower prices and better quality. Do not just be satisfied with a few.

Start Up Information For Complete Beginners

Your bouncy castle hire business can be successful if you have the enthusiasm, the drive, the passion and the willingness to learn from other people's mistakes. Take your time, do your homework and learn from those who have already become successful.

How To Ensure The Rain Does NOT Spoil The Bouncy Castle Party!
One of the biggest problems with hiring bouncy castles outdoors in temperate climates *(such as the UK)* is the unpredictable weather. One day it can be glorious sunshine, and your phone does not stop ringing. The next day it can be dark clouds and heavy rain. Unfortunately, heavy rain causes all sorts of problems for bouncy castle owners.

When the bouncy castle gets very wet, the children cannot use it for safety reasons, and if it has hardly been used, the customer may ask for a discount or even a full refund.

Most bouncy castles have rain-covers or shower-covers, but in prolonged heavy rain these tend to prove inadequate. How many times have you collected a castle after a very wet day, to find that not only is the rain cover soaking wet, but so is the inflatable? It then becomes a nightmare to try and get as much water off it as possible *(both inside and outside)*, and then to try and roll it up while it is still soaking wet.

Perhaps the biggest problem of all is trying to lift a very heavy soaking wet bouncy castle onto your sack trolley, and then trying to get it into your van when it can be nearly double the normal weight, because of all the rainwater inside.

Fortunately, there is a unique solution which goes a long way toward solving this problem of wet weather.

We will now look at this solution step-by-step

Step 1. In very wet weather rainwater gets sucked into the electric or petrol fan, and then gets forced deep inside the castle, adding enormously to the weight of the unit when it is rolled up, and coming up through the bed seams, when the castle is being used, and causing bubbles and froth. To prevent this rainwater being sucked into the blower, buy a plastic picnic table (approx. 4ft diameter) from any good DIY shop. If you then place this table over the fan, when it is raining, it will stop water from coming in the side vent, but still, allow the fan to suck air in.

Step 2. You will also need a heavy-duty rain cover that is oversized. For my 12ft x 12ft castles I buy a large piece of heavy duty tarpaulin (similar to what market traders use as a roof on their stalls) that measures about 8 metres x 8 metres (25ft x 25ft). I then lay this cover over the deflated castle. I then get a helper, or even the customer to hold one side of the cover, while I hold the other side. The fan is then switched on and as the castle inflates I make sure that the rain cover is evenly distributed over the castle.

Step 3. Once the castle is fully inflated, I then use string or twine to tie the rain cover to the metal stakes at each corner. The cover has eyelets spaced at intervals all the way around. As the rain cover is so oversized, it should seal up any gaps at the sides and back of the inflatable. (In moderately windy weather you may need an extra person to help hold the rain cover in place prior to its being tied down).

Step 4. At this stage, the rain cover should be securely attached to the castle, with no gaps showing. The front of the rain cover should be hanging loosely downwards, obscuring the bed of the castle. At this point get two telescopic keepnet poles which you can buy from your local fishing tackle shop, and press the sharp end into the ground, about 2 metres (7 feet) in front of the castle and to the left. Repeat this procedure with the other pole, but this time put it two metres (7 feet) out from the castle, but on the opposite side. I.e. on the right.

Step 5. Now take hold of the front of the rain cover, which is hanging downwards in a vertical position and move it outwards, so that it becomes about 45 degrees and forms an awning, which protrudes about 3 metres (10 feet) from the front of the castle. You then need to tie this awning to the two keepnet poles. Because the keepnet poles are adjustable, you can alter the angle of the awning. Providing everything is securely tied, the children should remain dry when using the castle.

IMPORTANT: Always make sure that any exposed electrics, e.g. plug sockets are fully protected by a waterproof bag, or better still, that waterproof connectors are used.

A few years ago I had an ideal opportunity to test this idea. To my amazement and delight, it worked extremely well. I recommend you do the same. If your castles already have good rain covers, I strongly recommend that at the very least you carry out step 1. I.e. putting a picnic table over the fan.

Inflatable Hire Disaster Preparation Kit
Hiring inflatables usually go very smoothly. However, at times, on rare occasions, there will be unexpected 'emergencies' such as a puncture or a breakdown or when a blower stops working or even if one loses their diary, or mallet while out delivering!

These types of 'emergencies' seem to always happen on the busiest weekend of the season! However, if you are aware of what these 'emergencies' and potential 'disasters' are likely to be, you can prepare for them and make contingency plans. The 15 most important items to carry in your 'disaster preparation kit' to cover you, should you have an 'emergency' are:

- Always carry a minor repair kit.
- Always carry a spare blower (especially if you travel a distance to your customer).
- Always carry a spare mobile phone battery (or cigarette charger).
- Always stake down the metal pegs so that the top is flush with the ground.
- Always carry a first aid kit.
- Always carry plastic fencing rolls.
- Always carry detergents and baby wipes for cleaning inflatables.

- Always carry a sheet of tarpaulin for rough gardens.
- Always ask the customer before the booking whether the inflatable will be sited on grass or concrete. (If on concrete take some sandbags).
- Use your mobile phone with a Google account for your diary. Some people prefer a paper diary, but you can lose them. Having your appointments saved in the cloud on a Google account means that you can access your appointments from anywhere in the world.
- Take two mallets in case one of your mallets is left behind at a customer's house or lost.
- Always carry spare 'Terms and Conditions' of hire forms.
- If it is windy or there are likely to be freak weather conditions, please use extra stakes, and ensure inflatable is switched off.
- Make sure that you are in the AA, RAC or Green Flag.
- Get an instant puncture repair kit - (silicon type substance in an aerosol can). Invaluable if you get a puncture on a busy hiring day.

Promoting Additional Services

It is a well-known fact that Amazon sells many more products (e.g. DVD's and books) than they would normally because at the bottom of each order page they have a list of RELATED products that they believe the customer will be interested in buying based on various buying trends from previous customers.

You can 'borrow' this idea to increase your hire profits. On the order page of your website have a section which reads:

"Customers who hired this item also hired an inflatable slide/sumo suits/assault course/garden games/etc." Also, have pictures underneath.

This just might encourage your customers to book ADDITIONAL items with you because they are not only reminded of these extra products that they can hire, at the point of purchase, but there is also a social proof element because other people hired them as well.

In addition, the actual words that Amazon uses, i.e. "Customers who bought this item also bought" (or similar) have proved to be extremely effective marketing.

I have never seen an inflatable hire company take advantage of this idea before.

More On Safety

Safety is a major concern for the inflatable hire industry. Fortunately, playing on inflatables is a very safe activity for children and adults providing basic precautions are put in place such as proper supervision by a responsible adult, and the inflatable being properly anchored down. Sometimes, however, there will be knocks and bruises, but this is normal when children are at play. From time to time, you do hear of accidents where the injuries are serious, and it hits the front pages of the national newspapers. The Health and Safety Executive (HSE), has published detailed guidelines to manufacturers and operators of such equipment. (See: en14960 below). This is one of the reasons why it is so crucial to have public liability insurance for your business.

The **Royal Society for the Prevention of Accidents** (ROSPA) has also issued guidelines for users. *Most of the injuries are caused by children bouncing off the inflatable onto the ground, being hit by other children or just falling awkwardly. Many of these accidents could be avoided by more effective and continuous adult supervision.* These notes are intended to give some guidance to those proposing to hire inflatable bouncy castles as part of a fund-raising event, a fete or a private function such as a birthday party.

The equipment should be hired from reputable hire companies, and wherever possible set up, operated and supervised by the hire company's own staff. This is particularly important if substantial numbers of children are likely to be present. Before hiring a bouncy castle, ensure that the hire company complies with the following guidelines.

1. Fully complies with the Health and Safety Executive (HSE) Guidance Notes: **EN 14960** (this important guide deals with all aspects of safety).

2. Employs suitably-experienced and trained adult personnel, where the company are responsible for the setting up, operation and supervision of the bouncy castle.

3. Provides written evidence of a current public liability insurance policy with a limit of indemnity of at least £2 million. This insurance is to cover the liability of the hire company.

4. If you are to operate the bouncy castle, in addition to Items 1 and 3 above, ensure that provision has been made for written instructions about the safe set up, operation and supervision of the equipment, and that the name and address of the manufacturer or supplier are clearly marked upon it. Beware of cheap 'toy' inflatables from catalogues, supermarkets, etc., as these are not suitable for parties.

The safety instructions should include the following points:-

- Children should not be allowed to use the bouncy castle if there is high wind or in wet weather (slippery surfaces may cause injury).
- The castle must be adequately secured to the ground using the correct anchor stakes.
- Soft matting covering hard surfaces must be placed adjacent to the front or open sides.
- There should be responsible adult supervision, paying close attention to the children at play at all times during its use.
- The number of children using the bouncy castle must be limited to the number recommended in the hire company's safety instructions. There must be no overcrowding.
- A rota system for different age or size groups should be operated, together with the observance of any age limit of users. (It is suggested that children over 12 years of age should not use the equipment).
- All children must be made to remove footwear, hard or sharp objects such as jewellery, buckles, pens and other similar pocket contents. Eating while bouncing or performing acrobatics must never be allowed.

(N.B. If you do not live in the United Kingdom, and you are thinking of operating bouncy castles, or hiring from a bouncy castle company, please check the legislation that is relevant to your particular country as it may be different from the UK's)

To emphasise the crucial importance of safety in a bouncy castle hire business, the BIHA has a written code of ethics (or code of conduct as some members may call it) which must be adhered to by all BIHA members. Also see: **http://www.biha.org.uk/code-of-ethics**

All BIHA members should follow a Code of Ethics. It is divided into a compulsory section and also a strongly recommended section.

Please note that the BIHA Code of Ethics is designed to not only make the industry safer but also to help operators run a more professional and profitable hire business. (Please also refer to the Standard: BS EN 14960 for more detailed information on Best Practice).

If a member deliberately violates this Code of Ethics (or refuses to comply), then they may forfeit their right to continue in membership, until they can prove that they can conform to the code as laid out below.

Compulsory
1. All inflatables must be visually inspected at the start of each hire for any rips, holes or bulges, or other signs of damage which could cause equipment failure.

2. All inflatables must be correctly staked down at all anchor points (usually minimum of 6) and guide ropes, where applicable, must be used. If the inflatable has to be sited on a hard surface such as concrete, wood or tarmac, then adequate heavy sand-bags (BS EN 14960 recommends 165 kg on EACH anchor point) must be attached to the anchor points to secure the inflatable. (Safety mats must also be used for entry/exit points when the inflatable is sited on a hard surface).

3. Every customer must be given a 'Terms and Conditions' of hire form and either a safety cartoon sheet or written safety/operating instructions (or similar). Every customer must be made aware of the maximum age (or height) and the maximum number of users permitted on the inflatable. Also, see form below which you can copy and show your customers.

4. Electrics must be PAT tested at REGULAR intervals. (This is normally recommended to be every 6 months -12 months*). This includes blowers, extension reels, RCD's and the electric mechanisms on rodeo bulls, etc.

THIS IS THE LAW. RCD's (power breakers) must always be used and installed at the source (not attached to the blower or extension reel socket).

5. Operators must NEVER hire out 'toy' or 'non-commercial' bouncy castles, slides or other 'toy' inflatables designed or classed for domestic use. These are not strong or robust enough for commercial hiring. Also, by doing so contravenes PUWER REGS (1998) and also the Health and Safety at Work Act (1974). Toy non-commercial inflatables are not built to the BS EN 14960 Standard, and in addition, they cannot be insured for public liability insurance purposes. So stay well clear!

6. Operators should always ensure that the age group of the users (e.g. children) is suitable for the size and type of inflatable. (e.g. a 12ft x 12ft bouncy castle is generally considered too small to accommodate teenagers).

7. Operators must always be polite and courteous to their customers, and other inflatable hire companies with whom they work.

8. In the event of windy weather (The Standard says, "wind speeds in excess of 24mph"), the inflatable must be switched off. The BIHA strongly recommends that each member invests in a hand-held Anemometer (costs approx. £30) to accurately measure wind-speed. If the inflatable is sited outdoors on a hard surface, then the Standard requires each weight at the anchor point to be 163 KG. (Yes, 163 kilogram's!). The inflatable must not be used in the event of heavy rain (light showers can be ignored) because they can become very slippery when wet.

9. Operators must always ensure that any exposed electrical connections are fully waterproofed prior to use. Use of specially designed waterproof outdoor electrical connections is best or special rain covers designed to cover the blower and the extension reel completely.

10. Operators must use a slip-sheet on inflatable slides (medium to large slides) to prevent users from falling through a split seam. (This requirement is not compulsory on some children's slides where the drop may be small (e.g. 3 -5 feet, or 1m -1.5m), although, it is *recommended* to have slip sheets on ALL slides.

11. Operators must never knowingly sell second-hand inflatables which are in a dangerous condition through any second-hand avenues, e.g. eBay.

12. Operators must ensure that responsible adults will be available to supervise children while playing on their inflatables.

13. All operators must have their inflatables tested by a 'competent person' at appropriate intervals (i.e. yearly). (The HSE view 'best practice' as being PIPA, RPII or ADIPS.)

Getting your inflatables tested annually is a legal requirement under PUWER REGULATIONS 1998. (Provision and Use of Work Equipment Regulations). See: http://www.hse.gov.uk/pubns/indg291.pdf The BIHA strongly recommend that this annual safety test is carried out by a PIPA or RPII registered tester -see: http://www.pipa.org.uk

Currently, the PIPA scheme (best practice) applies to bouncy castles, inflatable slides and any other non-domestic play inflatables used by children for bouncing and sliding. Please see: http://www.pipa.org.uk

Strongly Recommended

It is strongly recommended that operators provide rain-covers for their bouncy castles (especially when used by children). This provides protection from the rain and the sun.

It is strongly recommended that all operators buy Public Liability (PL) insurance for their inflatables. (£1m, £2m or £5m). Since March 2004 the cost has come down significantly. Operators who choose to run their business without PL insurance are being extremely unwise and to save a few pounds a year are playing a big risk with their personal finances. As PL insurance is now relatively cheap, all operators should ensure they have it. In addition, many local authorities and organisations insist that the operator has PL insurance in place before they will book an inflatable(s). It is strongly recommended that adequate safety mats are provided at the opening of each inflatable and at the bottom of slides. (N.B. If the inflatable is sited on a hard surface such as concrete, then providing safety mats at entry/exit points is compulsory)

* With regards to PAT Testing (See point 4 above) The 'Electricity at Work Regulations 1989' require that any electrical equipment that has the potential to cause injury is maintained in a safe condition. However, the Regulations do not specify what needs to be done, by whom or how frequently (i.e. they do not make inspection or testing of electrical appliances a legal requirement, nor do they make it a legal requirement to undertake this annually). Source: **http://www.hse.gov.uk/electricity/faq-portable-appliance-testing.htm** Also see: **http://www.biha.org.uk/code-of-ethics/**

The Law and 'Best Practice' for Operators of Inflatable Play Equipment

When a company, organisation or individual makes available any equipment in return for payment they become subject to the Health and Safety at Work Act 1974. This act places a duty of care on everyone involved in the transaction. This means that the operator, the operator's employees, the hirer, the hirer's employees and the owner or manager of the premises should do everything possible to ensure the safe use of the equipment.

In addition, Provision and Use of Work Equipment Regulations (PUWER) 1998 require that all work equipment and that includes inflatable play, must be tested by a competent person regularly (usually once a year).
THIS IS THE LAW.

However, in order to help inflatable hire companies comply with the law, the industry (in consultation with the Health and Safety Executive - HSE) introduced the Standard BS EN 14960 in 2006 and then revised it in 2013.
BS EN 14960:2013 Standard

As a bouncy castle hire company, your first priority must ALWAYS be the safety of the children and other users of your equipment. The BS EN14960 Standard covers all aspects of inflatable play equipment that is bounced or slide on. The standard was designed to ensure the safety of children and users and is currently BEST PRACTICE (i.e. not law).

The EN 14960 Standard was agreed upon by European Standardization Organizations, and the BSI Group and the HSE (Health and Safety Executive). It has the support of all the industry trade groups (including the BIHA). The Standard applies to the designing, manufacturing, inspecting and hiring out of inflatable play equipment. It was updated in 2006 and then again in 2013.

The Standard includes inflatable products where users either bounce on, slide on or both. When you buy an inflatable (either new or used) then it is extremely important that it conforms to the Standard in order to help maintain a safe playing environment for children.

The scope of the BS EN 14960:2013 standard
The European Standard is applicable to inflatable play equipment intended for use by children fourteen years and under both individually and collectively.

The Standard sets measures to address risks and to minimise accidents to users, in the design, manufacture and supply of inflatable play equipment. It specifies information to be supplied with the equipment. The requirements have been laid down bearing in mind the risk factor based on available data.

The standard specifies the requirements that will protect a child from hazards that he or she may be unable to foresee when using the equipment as intended, or in a manner that can be reasonably anticipated.

BS EN 14960 does NOT apply to inflatable swimming pool play and leisure equipment, domestic inflatable toys, air-supported buildings, inflatables used solely for protection, inflatables used for rescue, or other types of inflatable toys where the primary activity is not bouncing or sliding.

Introduction to BS EN14960:2013
'Play' is the means by which children discover and understand the world in which they live and is an essential element in a child's physical and mental growth.

It is very important for children's overall development that through play, they arrive at an understanding of danger, which provides a basis for assessing safety in a variety of situations. The balance between challenge and safety is an important consideration.

The inflatable play equipment referred to in the standard can provide different levels of challenge and excitement. The European Standard aims to minimise the level of risk and the possibility of serious injury while still allowing children to enjoy themselves when playing in or on inflatable equipment.

The standard acknowledges the difficulties of addressing safety issues by age criteria alone because the ability to handle risk is based on the individual user's level of skill and not age. Moreover, users other than the intended age range will make use of the inflatable equipment, in which case, the provisions of the standard still apply.

It is not the purpose of the requirements of the standard to affect a child's need to play nor to lessen the contribution that inflatable play equipment makes either to the child's development or meaningful play from an educational point of view.

Where inflatable play equipment is used with other items of children's playground equipment, the relevant standards applying to the other items of equipment should also be consulted.

BS EN14960:2013
Key points within the BS EN14960:2013 Standard include:

- Placement of the inflatable.
- Never near overhead obstructions such as trees or power lines.
- Never on a slope greater than 5%.
- Always upon a cleared area with no sharp objects or debris.
- Use a fence for the purposes of crowd control.
- Supervision.
- Users and equipment should always be supervised.
- Inflatables should be deflated when not in use, and the power source disconnected.
- Restriction on the number of users on the inflatable at any one time.
- Inflatable maintenance.
- Clean the inflatable.

- Take steps to avoid preventable repairs.
- Correct maintenance.
- Information to be supplied to the operators.
- Annual Inspection procedures.
- Operational procedures.
- How to safely set up the inflatable.
- Restrictions on use of the inflatable, e.g. users numbers and height.

These are just examples of the detail the Standard goes into, which are taken into account during the design and manufacture of inflatables which comply with the Standard.
To see more detail of the European Standard -please refer to **http://www.biha.org.uk/about-the-biha/en14960**

The European Standard for inflatable play equipment was published by the BSI in 2007.

The published standard is subject to copyright so cannot be made available on this page. It can only be purchased through the BSI - see **http://www.bsonline.bsi-global.com/server/index.jsp**.

In order to help inflatable hire companies and operators conform with the law and with 'best practice' the PIPA scheme was set up to help operators meet their obligations under Health and Safety legislation. The Health and Safety At Work, etc., Act 1974 and subsequent regulations require all inflatable play equipment that is, "designed to be used by members of the public for entertainment purposes either as a slide or for bouncing upon" to be tested at suitable intervals by a competent person.

Other types of device not covered by PIPA include:

> Devices classified as toys, devices designed for use in pools; privately owned devices which users do not pay to use.
> Source: **www.pipa.org.uk**
> Also see: RPII **http://rpii-inspectors.com**

Inspection by a competent person prior to first use and annually thereafter provides fundamental confidence in the equipment itself.

Operators using other testing schemes or methods may be required to demonstrate how such procedures equal or better the accepted 'best practice'. Testers with no formal qualifications, however well experienced, would probably not be able to satisfy a court of their competence to BS EN 14960.

Just to clarify a lot of people in the inflatable hire industry still think there are numerous laws governing it. There are not - virtually all the guidelines are 'best practice'! The only laws are the Health and Safety at Work Act 1974, (regarding Duty of Care as mentioned previously) and PUWER Regulations 1998 - which states that hire equipment must be tested at appropriate intervals by a competent person. (Furthermore, if you have employees, you MUST have Employers Liability Insurance). This is the Law! Everything else is 'Best Practice' although in the event of a child or other user being hurt on an inflatable, and the case going to court, the HSE (prosecuting) could use 'Best Practice' in order to ensure that 'A DUTY OF CARE' was upheld. In other words, the Standard can be used to ensure that the law was upheld. As previously mentioned, if an operator abides by PIPA or the RPII scheme it should satisfy the HSE that everything reasonably practical was done to ensure the safety of the users on the inflatables. If an operator chooses NOT to use PIPA, RPII or ADIPS they must prove to the court (and the HSE) that the 'scheme' they used was just as good. For this reason, the BIHA very strongly recommends all inflatable hire companies follow PIPA or RPII. The HSE also recognise the ADIPS scheme as fulfilling the requirements of the Standard, but ADIPS tends to be associated with very large inflatables used at Travelling Fun Fairs and similar events.

Also see some safety points at: **www.pipa.org.uk/pages/play-safe**

Are Bad Telephone Practices Hurting Your Bouncy Castle Hire Business?

Many bouncy castle owners spend hundreds of pounds on marketing and promotional activities each month to attract more customers. Yet all this effort and expense can be wasted if a potential customer telephones your business and hangs up with a less than positive impression of how the call was handled. Here are four easy ways to quickly improve your telephone skills or those of your staff to help ensure that you always get the booking.

1. Start the call right. Ensure your phone is answered promptly whenever possible. It is not always feasible to have a backup person available to answer the phone, so remind your staff that a ringing telephone is everyone's business. Also, start the call right by having a telephone answering script so that everyone answers the telephone in a consistent manner. An example might be, "Good afternoon, this is the ABC Bouncy Castles. My name is John". (People are more comfortable when they know whom they are talking). "How may I help you?" indicates a desire to serve.

2. Provide a 'cheat sheet'. At some point, 90 per cent of callers will ask for the same information, such as what size of bouncy castle do they need, what age group is suitable for each type of inflatable. The other important item of information they will want is the price of hiring your bouncy castle out. You will have this on the cheat sheet, but of course, you need to check that you have a suitable unit available for hire to them before quoting a price. Keep a list of typical questions and well-crafted responses by each telephone in your home or office.

3. Ask the caller questions so that you can more easily gauge their needs. E.g. ask them how many children they are planning to invite and what the ages of the children are. What type of event is being celebrated? Build a rapport with the caller BEFORE you start reeling off a load of prices or quotes. You are also checking that you have the right bouncy castle to hire to the caller. There is no point setting a cheap children's inflatable up at a low price when the customer states that it is for a teenager's party. The whole hire is doomed from the start.

4. Train yourself and your staff to talk with a SMILE! This might seem too simple, but one of the most important elements in making a positive phone impression is speaking with a smile. Callers actually "hear" the smile in the tone and style of a person's voice. A friendly voice with a smile puts your callers at ease and tells them they have selected the right bouncy castle hire company with whom to do business.

5. Always be professional in the way you deal with people who call your business. Do not use colourful language and do not criticise your competitors when discussing other company's prices. Over time you will learn that a confident and professional phone response will often get you the business ahead of another company who are less professional.

Your Business Website

Ten years ago there were still some businesses which were not sure if they should have a website. Now it is seen as imperative to any business, and that includes your bouncy castle business. If the thought of sorting this out terrifies you then do not worry. The BIHA has recommended internet experts who can set your website up and keep it going at very reasonable prices.

Your inflatable hire business deserves the same amount of attention as any other business - large or small. Technological advances in a world that never pauses now enable every small business to compete with large corporations, and having a website is an extremely affordable way to market your small business.

Still not sure about this?

Here I have compiled a list of the top 10 reasons why you need a website:

1. Increase Customer Potential
A web site will explain your services to a larger number of prospective customers and increase the size of your targeted customer base. The website will make your business available to a larger number of consumers and expose your products and services to a greater variety of potential customers. Effective internet usage creates many bridges by using social networks, directories, and advertising that all point back to your destination - a well designed, well-written, website.

If you think about how you use your mobile phone, how many times have you done a search for a local business to make a call? Unless you are a dinosaur, you know that this is the way most business contacts are made in the twenty-first century. So you need to be listed on the search engines when people look for *'bouncy castle hire'* on their mobiles. Most even have a *'Companies near your location'* feature which will actually help you win business if you are the nearest address to your potential customer.

2. Increase Your Profile

With a website, customers see your business as more professional, dynamic, modern, and better able to serve their needs. Businesses without a website are often perceived by potential customers as small and inept. Even worse, a business with a mundane web page design will seem uncertain and unprofessional. What will potential customers think if your competitors all have a beautiful website and all you have is a Facebook page?

The current trend is for very simple clean-looking websites. They must provide only critical information on the screen -your business, your location and your phone number. All other information is superfluous as far as mobile search is concerned. Of course, you will have lots of other information on your website, but for the customer looking for quick and easy answers, you need to give them a reason to call you. So make it easy for them with a professional good looking mobile website.

3. Your website will promote your business 24/7

Having talked about mobile websites in section two above, you still need to have a full website for people who are on Tablet computers, desktop computers and laptops. If you plan correctly, this will be the same website which can be easily read on all devices.

Customers can access your website 24 hours a day, seven days a week. It is always available to them. This is great if you have a customer who does hours of research before making a call to book a hiring. They can read about your products and services when it is convenient for them--quite often, long after you have locked up and gone home. They can also browse through testimonials from previous customers; this is a powerful page in helping potential customers make up their mind.

An effective website design can efficiently answer customer enquiries all day and night, not to mention - take bookings while you are asleep! (See: www.BouncyCastleNetwork.co.uk/biha for excellent online booking software) You will need to make all automated bookings subject to a suitability questionnaire, but if you have regular customers, online bookings are great.

4. Attract Prospects Ahead of the Competition

For many people, the purchasing decision starts by researching inflatable hire services using the web. Purchasing decisions are made long before the first phone call or online booking. Become a part of the consumers' research process with an effective website design. Put as many elements on your website as possible.

These can include videos of how to use a bouncy castle safely, a welcoming video with you talking to the camera about how you can help your customer have a successful party event. You should use lots of pictures of people enjoying your castles from previous hirings. You cannot beat a happy smiling child's face for 'feel-good' factor. If you have had some media coverage, then make sure this has a section somewhere on the website. I know a company who won a business start-up competition run by a local radio station. The owner was interviewed, and the interview was placed on the website. This added credibility for this new business and the website had a lot of attention through this event.

5. Increase Popularity Using Social Media

Providing a well-designed website complements social networking sites like Facebook and Twitter. Using a website to engage prospective customers by offering exclusive discounts to a specific social network will gain popularity unheard of in any other medium. A website puts you in control of the ordering process.

Ask customers to 'Like' your Facebook page. If they are happy with your service, they will not mind the request. You can also build a special Facebook page for your business, though do not let this detract from your main website. Some businesses offer flash sales by tweeting them to followers using Twitter. So if you have a quiet week with no hiring booked, you could tweet the following:

"Book our Bouncy Castle for your party this weekend and make it go with a swing! #Bouncy Castle Party" This could result in you getting a hire when you had nothing better to do. It does not cost a great deal of money. Just a bit of time on your part.

6. Target Potential Customers
Customers who visit your website are interested in your services. They have found your site via Google, or you shared it on Twitter, Facebook or other social networking sites. They are ready to make a purchasing decision. Your business promotion is effective when your website is viewed by interested potential customers.

Some businesses target specific customer groups on their websites. So you could decide that you want to have a 'Bouncy Castles For Playgroups' page. Or 'Schools Special Services' for people with learning difficulties. Your only limit is your imagination here. I would choose a sector that I have some experience in so that I sound knowledgeable when the call comes in to make a booking. Customers talk to each other, and once you get a reputation in a certain sector of the market, you become the leader of the pack for it over time.

7. Establish Credibility
We have already touched on this in the points above, but it is worth reiterating. Answer customer queries and share valuable information that goes beyond simply selling your service by providing compelling content on your website. Customer's value detailed information and an informative website denoting the business as knowledgeable and professional.

You need to engage customers on your website, so quality and informative content is a must. Being a member of the BIHA will allow you to display the association logo which will add to your professional look. See Later section -35 Credibility Factors

8. Increase Communication with Customers
Use your website to serve as a catalyst for your business by further engaging customers from popular social networking sites to close the deal

on your business website. Online-forms may also be used so that customers can request more information or place orders.
(See: www.BouncyCastleNetwork.com)

9. Advertise Inexpensively
Technological advances have made small business web development more affordable than ever before. Spruce up your advertising through affordable web design and receive a greater return on your investment when compared to the cost of advertising on radio and television, in newspapers, or in the Yellow Pages.

In the 1990's you could not consider not using paper directories such as Thomson and Yellow Pages. In a previous business, I used to have a half-page advertisement costing £9,000 per year in my local directory. Crazy price! It worked then, but it does not work now. No one uses these paper directories. Instead, they use online search engines, so you need your business to be there loud and proud. And once you are set up the costs for continuing your online presence is tiny by comparison.

10. Market Effectively
Website design does not limit the volume of content that you can present to potential customers. Other types of promotional media (such as print, radio, and television) charge fees by the word or second. A six-page website allows you to fully explain your business services. You can tell potential customers about your staff, qualifications, existing clients, previous bookings, or just about anything that will benefit your business.

For more details about how to use your website to get more bookings, please read Volume 2 'Internet Marketing for Bouncy Castle Hire Companies -How To Double Or Triple Your Bookings And Profits Using The Power Of The Internet'.

The pages you should include on your website are as follows:

Home Page -A short, sharp and attractive call to action. You want people to make the call.

About Us -More information about who you are and how you can help your customers.

Testimonials -Customers are usually willing to give positive testimonials

You should place these on a special page. Do not alter the wording in any way; leave them exactly as they are given to you.These three pages are enough for a new start-up business. Once you have the time and the money you can increase your content.

Note: There is a current EU directive that means you must ask the website visitor's permission to use cookies on your website site. You will have seen them on all websites in the last few years. This is easy and low cost (or free) to set up, so do not worry.

How To Skyrocket Your Bookings By Uploading Videos Of Your Bouncy Castles Onto YouTube.com

It has been proved that by putting photographs of your bouncy castles and other inflatables onto your website, business cards, vans, etc., more people will book them for their parties. However, what is not so well-known is that putting videos of your bouncy castles (in use) onto YouTube can generate even more excitement (and bookings) from your clients and prospective clients! But how exactly do you do it? This brief article will show you in 7 easy steps how to upload your video onto YouTube which should see your bookings increase if you put the YouTube video link on your website.

It has been proven that by putting photographs of your bouncy castles and other inflatables onto your website, business cards, vans etc., will attract more people to book them for their parties and events. However, what is not so well known is that putting a video of your bouncy castles in action on YouTube can generate even more excitement (and bookings) from your clients and prospective clients! But how exactly do you do it? This brief article will show you in 7 easy steps how to upload your video onto YouTube and see your bookings increase if you put the YouTube video link on your website.

You do not need a fancy expensive video camera to record your videos. Most smartphones have excellent video cameras included. These will take perfectly acceptable videos for your YouTube account. Of course, if you are the owner of an expensive camera, then, by all means, use it. It is not a necessity, however.

Step 1: Become a member of YouTube
By going to the signup page on the YouTube website and create a username and password. If the username you are attempting to create is already taken, the words "username unavailable" will appear beside your entry. You will have to try another. Because YouTube is now owned by Google, they will try to link up any Google account you might have with your YouTube account. You might want to keep your business separate from your private life, which is fine. Just be careful as you sign up to keep your information separate.

Step 2: Confirmation Email
YouTube will send you a confirmation email. Check your email and click the link provided to verify you submitted the correct email address.

Step 3: Upload Video
Go to the YouTube website. Find and click the "Upload Videos" link in the upper right-hand corner of your computer screen.

Step 4: Video Details
Type details and descriptions about your video. Title your video. Include a description of its contents. Decide on tags for your video. These are the keywords that will pull up your video when searched for by other users. Do not forget to pick the best category for your video.

Step 5: Find Your Video on your computer
Select "Continue Uploading" at the bottom of the page. Then click "Browse" and locate the video on your computer that you want to upload.

Step 6: Select Video
Click on the video you want to upload, then click "Open." Choose if you would like your video to be available to the public, or if you want only chosen friends and family to see it. Select "Upload Video" to start the process of transferring from your computer to the YouTube website.

Step7: Wait for Upload to complete
Allow up to five minutes for every megabyte of your video. This time can be faster or slower, depending on your connection type.

For further instructions on how to upload your videos to YouTube simply follow the tutorials provided on the YouTube website itself. They are clear and comprehensive.

You Must Have A Mobile-friendly Website -But it can be the same site as your main website
I have already discussed the importance of planning your website to be mobile-friendly earlier in this section. But here are some of the reasons behind this.

Why Your Website Must Be Mobile Friendly (Now More Than Ever!)

Did you know that four out of five people now use smartphones and tablets to shop? (Including looking for a bouncy castle or other inflatable to hire)

Let us face it, nowadays just simply having a website is no longer enough for your business to truly connect with consumers online. More than ever, your potential customers are using mobile devices to search for inflatable hire businesses in their area and to shop online.

Having a mobile website can make a big difference in how many customers find and interact with your business. The use of mobile phones to browse the internet is not new, but it continues to rise dramatically, making a mobile website more and more important for businesses who wish to stay ahead of their competitors.

Why being Mobile Friendly Is Important for Your Hire Business.
Studies show that the average consumer is spending more time browsing and utilizing the web on a mobile device than on a desktop or laptop. Tablets and phones can be conveniently carried around and accessed instantly. How often have you seen someone looking at their phone while waiting for a bus, sitting in a restaurant, or taking a break from work? All of those moments are opportunities for your business if you have a mobile-friendly website.

Some Statistics to Think About:
In a 2014 study, advertising network InMobi found that in the UK people are spending more time accessing the internet through their mobile devices than through their PCs. This means that if your business's website is designed only for PCs, you are missing out on over half of the market! Furthermore, about one in three online searches are now conducted through mobile devices. People use their phones when they are out and about and looking for a local service. If your website comes up in their search results and is easy to access, you might gain an immediate new customer.

A recent study by iAcquire found that 70% of mobile online searches result with an action taken within less than an hour of the search. This means that mobile searches are a more effective way of reaching customers than desktop searches, and can quickly result in new customer interactions and sales.

Connect with Customers Where They Already Are.
Nowadays it is pretty much second nature for just about everyone to use their phone to access the internet. No matter where your customer is, simply by having a website that is easy to access on a mobile device, you are making it easier for customers to browse your website and find what they need and take the next action.

Whether it is your business phone number, information about your hire products etc., they can browse your website with ease and quickly find what they are looking for - and that is the bottom line! Mobile websites make it easier for consumers to get the information they want.

Free Ways To Get More Business
Over the years a few new BIHA members have complained to me that they cannot get many bookings for their inflatables.

Someone who is a brand-new start-up may be competing directly with well-established hire companies who perhaps have flooded the area with advertising in the past and now get the bulk of their work from repeat business and word of mouth referrals, etc.

I have also had comments from both new members and old members alike that having a good website (with a high Google ranking) and an active Facebook page is bringing in a reasonable level of business for them, but there is still much room for improvement, especially for lucrative events and weekday bookings, etc.

Fortunately, children are born every day of the week in your area, so demand for inflatable hire will not go away any time soon!

Listed below are some alternative (and some may say 'old-fashioned') ways of promoting your hire business outside the realm of your website and your Facebook page.

Some of these ideas will be 'old-hat' to you, whilst others will be a timely reminder of 'forgotten' marketing tips and ideas to get you more bookings throughout the entire year -not just in the peak season!

Leaflet Distribution
Get a few thousand leaflets printed, and then contact other companies (or agencies) which do leaflet distribution, and ask for a shared leaflet drop. A way to save money is to approach your local Pizza/Chinese/Indian takeaway, and tell them that you will deliver their leaflets for free if they

pay for your printing costs! Crafty, but it works! Get another fast-food company involved, and you could make a small profit by delivering leaflets which could contribute to your other advertising and marketing costs.

Children's Groups
Contact every school, nursery, playgroup, childminder, PTA, Scout Groups, Brownie groups, Youth Clubs, After-School groups, children's charities, family attraction centres, zoos, farms, etc., which cater for families, in your LOCAL area. Then tell them that you would be delighted to loan them a FREE bouncy castle for the day or half-day (FOR FUND-RAISING PURPOSES - make sure you mention this as you may be taken much more SERIOUSLY by the person in charge of the group. They can hardly say "no" to you - if it will help raise urgently needed funds).

In return for your providing a FREE bouncy castle for the day, they need to allow you to give out flyers to all the parents and children in attendance.

Corporate Market
For the lucrative corporate market, a similar version of this idea can also be effective. Contact the Social Secretary of large and Blue Chip Companies in your local area, and offer to donate a free inflatable for the day, with the idea that any funds raised will go to their chosen charity. If they jump at the chance, you can then contact your local newspaper who may well send a reporter to cover the event. All of a sudden, you have FREE newspaper advertising worth hundreds of pounds or more. A very happy charity, and hopefully a very happy company which may well use your services for future lucrative corporate events.

When I did this, I also found that I received food and other goodies throughout the course of the day. If you are too busy to attend in person, ask someone from the charity to help. They may even want to have a stand.

When using this approach, adopt the mindset of FUND-RAISING, and you should be richly rewarded for your actions. In addition, you should get referrals from the parents in attendance. Furthermore, the word may spread to other companies in your LOCAL area who are interested in hiring inflatables from you.

Links With Businesses
This can be extremely powerful. Contact other local companies in the party and events industry such as your local party shop, your local face-painter, marquee-hirer, children's entertainer, event organiser, etc., and tell them that you would like to refer your customers to them if they can return the favour! And also share mailings. (One entrepreneurial BIHA member even helped to organise a consortium of local companies to supply the various services and equipment for the weddings in his town, via the local party/wedding shop).

Combine With Your Competitors
This is a similar idea, which some may disagree with. Get to know your local competitors! And get friendly with them! Find out what equipment they have, and what they do *not* have. For example, they may only rent out corporate play inflatables for the adult market and are continuously turning away potential customers enquiring after children's bouncy castles, or vice versa.

Shop Windows
This idea is not usually considered - even by established inflatable hire companies. It is extremely simple and merely involves taking a photograph of your best and brightest bouncy castle or other play inflatable, printing it, gluing it onto a postcard (with your contact details at the top) and then putting it in the window of your local busy newsagents or post-offices, (Costs around £1 per week). Some supermarkets and hairdressers, etc., also let you do this for free!

Virtually no-one else who advertises in shop windows does this, so your photographic advertisement will be very prominent in the newsagent's window. (Have you seen how some people just scribble out an advertisement and it is almost impossible to read?)

Promotional Clothing
Buy some quality clothing (e.g. Jackets, T-shirts, Sweatshirts, polo-jumpers, base-ball caps, etc.) and then have your company logo and contact details printed on them. I have known situations where a BIHA member has been in a queue to pay for diesel, and someone behind them has tapped them on the shoulder and told them that they want to hire a bouncy castle from them, just because their name and logo was on the back of their jacket. Very rewarding and means that waiting in a queue with several people around can actually be profitable -and it is free!

Business Cards and Flyers
Always carry your business cards and flyers with you. You never know who you will meet while you are out and about! There are some instances where a local public centre (e.g. your local library, community centre, veterinary surgery, doctor's surgery, etc.) will allow you to place your flyers free of charge).

Newspaper Features
Local newspapers are frequently interested in featuring local business people and their accomplishments. This is free advertising and if the opportunity arises should always be used. You can also contact your local community magazine and offer to write a monthly or weekly guest column for them, and include your author bio and website URL.

Asking For Referrals
It goes without saying that every time you accept a booking, you should be asking the customer for referrals. If you feel uncomfortable asking them directly, then you can do it indirectly, For example, give them vouchers to distribute to their friends, relatives and neighbours. I have even heard of members who will pay a small commission to their customers if they refer them to new customers such as: "Get a free bouncy castle for every 10 new customers who you refer to us."

Approach HR Departments
Write to the social secretary or HR Department of local businesses and make them aware of your services. Even better, make an appointment to

and visit them. Many medium-to-large companies have family fun days in the summer, team-building events and other corporate events throughout the year.

Community Groups
Get involved in your LOCAL community. Look for groups and associations that align with your priorities and values, e.g. your local Chamber of Commerce. Volunteerism is a great way to 'network' as well. I knew somebody who connected with the local Asian community in his town. He did a good job, and within weeks had more than enough work to keep him busy during the season.

Car Signs
Get a magnetic sign made for your car as well as your business. For the one-time cost of the sign, your business name will be on display everywhere you drive. (Do not cut people up though!). Many hire companies have elaborate sign-written vans but forget to advertise their hire business on the side and/or back of their *car!*

Reviews for Other Businesses
Write good reviews for local businesses and send them off to them via snail-mail or email. Local businesses appreciate positive reviews, and the more they have on the internet and in their brochures and flyers, etc., the better. So help out your local businesses by being a good customer, then getting online and writing about your experiences. You will gain favour from your fellow-business owners and potential customers who are researching local businesses. They will keep seeing your name appear and, of course, the name of your *inflatable hire business.*

Regular Newsletter
Start a FREE monthly (or quarterly) newsletter to all your customers and people who express an interest in your hire services. This can be done by post using the Royal Mail, but Email Newsletters also work. See later tip for more information.

Recruit Affiliates

You can use 'affiliates' to help you get more bookings. There are plenty of 'stay-at-home mums', students, fit retired people, etc., who would be more than happy to get bookings for you using some of the above methods, in return for a commission on each hire. If you are worried that this might eat into your hire profits too much, simply increase your booking fee by say £3 to £5 to take this commission aspect into account.

Online Marketing

A book on how to start and run a profitable bouncy castle hire business would not be complete without a chapter on online marketing and getting many customers from the internet. However, just a chapter on this vitally important topic is not enough, and so we have dedicated an entire book on the subject which is Volume 2 in this series. 'Internet Marketing for Bouncy Castle Hire Companies - How to Double or Triple Your Profits Using The Power of The Internet'.

Volume 2 is a must-read, breakthrough book written specifically for inflatable hire companies in the UK and the Republic of Ireland.
Here are some of the topics covered in depth in Volume 2:

- Why the internet is so important for bouncy castle hire companies.
- What tools (free and paid) are available for you to take maximum advantage of the internet.
- Step-by-step SEO techniques to get your website ranking at the top of the Search Engines.
- Having a top ranking website is just 50% of the battle. The other 50% is converting visitors into customers and clients.
- Why your website must look good on a mobile device, and how you can pick up extra bookings from customers on the move.
- Why you should consider an online booking system and how it can not only reduce your workload but also increase profits considerably and your enjoyment of the hire business.
- The correct way to optimize your website for 'Google Maps', now called 'Google My Business'.
- The crucial importance of Social Media marketing for your inflatable hire business.
- Why customer reviews are so important, and the best type of review that will get you more bookings.
- Do not forget to include video on your website! TWO massive reasons you should, and it is much easier than you think to do.
- And much, much more…

To order a copy of 'Internet Marketing for Bouncy Castle Hire Companies - How to Double or Triple Your Profits Using The Power of The Internet' please visit the BIHA website at **www.biha.org.uk**

82 Other Blunders Which Could Damage Your Bouncy Castle Hire Business

Here are 82 blunders and mistakes that some inflatable hire companies (even established ones) and that could have done serious harm to their business, reduced their profits or even, in the long run, destroyed it! These blunders must be identified and avoided to ensure a healthy business which can become more and more profitable. They are:

1) Forgetting to join the BIHA Facebook group. Web address - **www.facebook.com/groups/biha4u**. You can post any question or problem-related to hiring bouncy castles and inflatables, and you should normally expect a reply within a few hours.
2) Not asking for referrals
3) Not joining the BIHA. See: **www.biha.org.uk**
4) Having an amateurish website
5) Not accepting PayPal
6) Not accepting credit cards
7) Not having your van 'sign-written'
8) Spelling mistakes and grammatical errors in your sales copy
9) Forgetting to contact the customer to confirm a booking
10) Not having a spare backup blower
11) Not carrying a 'tyre weld' or a spare wheel
12) Forgetting to carry a first aid kit
13) Failure to get friendly with your competitors
14) Forgetting to have two diaries (one as a backup)
15) Naming your company using the *end* letters of the alphabet, e.g. Zebedee's Bouncy Castle Hire.
16) Forgetting to renew your domain name
17) Having too long an e-mail address
18) Not having a USP (Unique Selling Proposition), i.e. why should a customer use you instead of a competitor?

19) Not taking adequate precautions with storing inflatables to guard against theft, e.g. padlocks not being strong enough
20) Not checking e-mails regularly enough
21) Not backing up your emails and data onto a portable hard drive or flash key drive, etc.
22) Not taking pictures of your bouncy castles and inflatables to put on your website
23) Forgetting to wear corporate clothing with your logo on the back!
24) Forgetting to collect a customer's e-mail address
25) Forgetting to e-mail customers when you have their e-mail address
26) Forgetting to optimise your website for the search engines (especially Google)
27) Not having the occasional day off or mini-break during the summer
28) Not delegating enough
29) Trying to run the business single-handed, which can cause burn out
30) Sending mail by 2nd class when you should use 1st class
31) Using a sack trolley which does NOT have pneumatic tyres
32) Using poor quality stationery
33) Forgetting to outsource routine jobs
34) Working too hard
35) Sending information packs off in A3 size and using the wrong postage stamps, resulting in unhappy customers who have to pay the excess to the Royal Mail (Revenue Protection). Make sure you use A5 envelopes if required, and with the requisite stamps
36) Paying too much for disposables and consumables. Shop around for printer ink, cleaning pads for castles, etc., - Tesco's is often the cheapest
37) Forgetting to ring the customer the night before to confirm the booking
38) Being overweight and/or unfit. When hiring out inflatables, you need to be in tip-top physical condition or the job will be that extra bit harder
39) Getting an amateur to do your website for you

40) Forgetting to thank customers for their business
41) Not having a plan
42) Not having clearly defined goals
43) Leaving your mobile switched off
44) Using a mobile phone whilst driving and not using a blue-tooth or hands-free kit
45) Forgetting to get customers to sign a disclaimer
46) Forgetting to use the BIHA cartoon safety sheet
47) Forgetting to use the 'Terms and Conditions' of hire forms
48) Not registering for a free copy of 'Inflated News' magazine
49) Not having another source of income
50) Having poor quality graphics on your website
51) Forgetting to provide smart uniforms for your employees
52) Forgetting to stake the bouncy castle down correctly
53) Not being creative enough, e.g. some hire companies will provide a fancy dress for their employees for that added 'wow factor'
54) Forgetting to properly dry out bouncy castles/inflatables after they get wet
55) Forgetting to use talcum powder sprinkled on the inflatable to help prevent the build-up of mildew and smells, before it is stored away
56) Forgetting to put crash mats at the front and sides of the inflatable
57) Falling victim to web scams and e-mail scams
58) Forgetting to add words of praise or testimonials to your website. The easiest way to get a testimonial is to provide a free bouncy castle to a school, playgroup or nursery. (Ideally ask for lots of referrals as well)
59) Forgetting to ask the customer to measure their garden
60) Forgetting to ask the customer the ceiling height for an indoor booking
61) Forgetting to tell the customer that your castles are clean and hygienic
62) Not washing the balls from the ballpond
63) Not backing up the sim card on your mobile phone

64) Forgetting to carry a spare mallet in your van (if you leave your only mallet behind at a customer's house, you will have to go back to collect it).
65) Forgetting to check when your website domain name expires
66) Forgetting to check when your van or car MOT expires
67) Forgetting to check when your van or car tax or insurance expires
68) Not having a backup job sheet (this could be kept in your wallet for safe keeping)
69) Not charging the customer a deposit for putting the balls back in the ball pond
70) Not providing a rain cover
71) Forgetting to join the AA or the RAC in case of break-down.
72) Being a perfectionist! Instead, 'do it first, perfect it later'
73) Not running a diesel van (petrol vans cost a lot more to run)
74) Not getting to know the caretakers of community halls
75) Not asking your customers for testimonials
76) Not looking at opportunities in the corporate market
77) Having a too long domain name: (e.g. **www.johnsmithsbouncycastlehirecompany.com**, if your competitor has **www.jsleiesure.com**.) Make it easy for your customers to enter your name in a browser
78) Forgetting to check your junk mail or spam folder for missing bookings
79) Using a non-geographical telephone number, e.g. 0870/0800 which could be controversial and could cause you to lose bookings, as a potential customer might think that the company they are phoning is *not* local.
80) Not keeping a close eye on business expenses and keeping costs down
81) Not using an accountant
82) Not being courteous and polite to your customers and competitors and staff

35 Credibility Factors For Your Bouncy Castle Business

There are 35 'Trust and Credibility' factors you can add to your inflatable hire business today to attract more customers.

Persuade your potential customers to TRUST you more BEFORE they contact you to make a booking or enquire about prices, etc.

There are many different ways of acquiring that trust, and they all involve adding a few words or some images to your website and to your business stationery (e.g. letterheads and business cards) and your marketing materials such as flyers.

It amazes me how few BIHA members actually take advantage of these 'TRUST FACTORS' which can have a huge positive psychological effect on your customers before they even contact you to book an inflatable!

I have made a list of what I consider to be the main 35 'TRUST FACTORS'.

TRUST AND CREDIBILITY FACTORS for inflatable hire companies:

1) Add testimonials and reviews (Use real people's names, addresses and photographs if possible - not: Mrs A from Manchester -- which looks like it is just made up! and your potential customers will see straight through it!) Video testimonials from genuine happy customers are the most powerful testimonials of all!
2) Mention when you launched your company, particularly if it was some years ago. E.g. "Established 1995" or "Hiring bouncy castles continually since 2002", or "delighting children continually since 2006".
3) If you have been featured in your local newspaper or on TV mention this fact. Creates instant credibility!

4) Mention on your website that you are a member of the BIHA. (Do not just add the BIHA logo shield). Instead, actually let visitors know that you are a BIHA *member*. Official research has found that 94% of the general public feel more confident about contacting a company (e.g. an inflatable hire business) who is a member of a recognised industry trade body. (Source: MORI)

5) Include a photograph of you and your staff or team on your website and marketing materials. (Creates a more personal feel). FACT: People buy people first BEFORE they buy products or services. This is well worth remembering.) Some companies have a page on their website dedicated to their team. This might include a photograph of each team member and a short bio of them. It has been proven scientifically that if you have pictures of yourself on your website and other promotional materials, customers and prospective customers will trust you more (be it a large team or a small husband-and-wife-team, for example).

6) Include a short video of your inflatables on your website to an appealing soundtrack (and upload to YouTube) to "wow" your potential customers. (If you do not know how to do this, please post on the forum) To see an example of a video click on http://youtu.be/0P0G13571kE, Please look at the videos on the BIHA homepage at www.biha.org.uk

7) If true, mention that you have full public liability insurance for 'peace of mind'.

8) If true, mention that you have spare vans and spare drivers in case of an emergency.

9) If true, mention that you have children of your own, so that you realise the vital importance of reliability and punctuality.

10) If true, mention that you and your staff are fully DBS checked.

11) If true, mention that you are a family-run business.

12) If true, mention that there is no cancellation charge for wet or windy weather (Gives your prospective customers peace of mind).

13) If true, mention that your inflatables are PIPA or RPII registered.

14) Give the FULL name and address of your business. This helps customers trust you more, and also Google will tend to rank you

higher in their Places Listing for LOCAL searches. (I am aware that some members prefer to hide their address details for fear of theft. This is understandable, but you need to be aware that Google may penalise your business and rank you in a lower position because it does not know precisely where you are based when someone searches for a "bouncy castle in their local town".)

15) Mention your 'opening hours' for each day of the week. (Many members including highly experienced hire companies forget to do this. It builds trust, and also Google likes it!)

16) Give your prospective customers multiple points of contact (e.g. mobile, text, email, landline). All customers have their PREFERRED method of contact which may be different from yours!

17) If you are able to take PayPal and credit cards, then display these symbols on your website and marketing materials. These logos have an extremely high trust-factor when people see them. Experts on this subject even go as far as saying that when people see these logos, it actually puts them in a 'buying mood', because many people regard credit card money as not real money, but 'funny money' or 'monopoly money'. E.g. the plastic pays for it! Also, credit card logos on your website adds professionalism to your business.

18) Have a Frequently Asked Questions (FAQ) page. Put your customers' minds at rest by answering their most searching questions before or after they have spoken to you.

19) Include photographs of your best inflatables preferably above the fold (I.e. in the top section of your website, before a visitor needs to scroll down). Some members forget to include this vital trust factor.

20) Include some scarcity. E.g. "In the summer we tend to become very busy, so please book your bouncy castle early to avoid disappointment."

21) Get a Facebook Business page, and also consider a Twitter, Google+1 account and Linked-In, and LINK them to your website. Google will reward you for having these and should rank your website higher up in its listings. Also, your trust factor with customers and potential customers will be higher. So it is worth doing?

22) Add a weather forecast to your website.

23) Check your website has the correct year at the footer and other crucial areas. Some bouncy castle hire websites I have seen have "new inflatables for 2012" on them, or even worse - "new for 2010". This just might prevent a potential customer from calling you -- as they may think your website is redundant or out of date!

24) Add a blog to your website - Google will love it - and rank you higher - FACT!

25) If you do not yet have a website - please get one! Otherwise, you are literally leaving money on the table. You build immediate trust and credibility in the eyes of potential customers when they can see pictures of your inflatables and customer reviews, etc. If you do not yet have a website, the BIHA strongly recommend www.BouncyCastleNetwork.com , with basic search engine optimization (SEO) built in (to get you onto that all-important page 1 ranking in Google).

26) If you have attended an RPII Operators Training Course, then tell your prospective customers! They may not have a clue as to what it is, but the fact that you have been on a formal training course adds credibility. To find out when the next RPII Training Course is - please contact the RPII at **www.playinspectors.com**

27) If you hire out a fairly large number and variety of inflatables, then you should seriously consider investing in an online booking system. The BIHA strongly recommend Bouncy Castle Network (www.bouncycastlenetwork.com). Sometimes, a customer will be planning their child's party at 10pm (or later) when they have time after a busy day. They may feel uncomfortable about telephoning a hire company at that time. However, with an online booking system, they can book anytime they like - at their own convenience. This is a big Trust Factor!

28) Check your website for spelling mistakes! This is a not a major issue, but if one of your potential customers sees a spelling mistake or two, it can appear unprofessional. They may think "Well, if they can't take care of the spelling, then what guarantee do I have that they will take care of my booking." Perhaps this is a bit extreme, but some people are very fussy about spelling and expect people to get it right first time.

29) Put your prices up. (Or alternatively, have a higher price option, e.g. an elite or super-deluxe price). If your prices are too low, especially if they are cheaper than your competitors, some potential customers may assume that your professionalism and quality of inflatables and service, etc., are inferior.

30) Have an informative "About Us" page. An "About Us" page is a good opportunity for you to give as much information as possible, to help you get more customers. Include a photograph of yourself and your team members. Mention why you started an inflatable hire business, etc. Perhaps include a short video of you welcoming visitors to your website. (See point # 35 for more details on this)

31) Get high-quality images of happy children, (especially where they are looking directly at the camera) and put them at the top of your marketing materials and of your website - alongside photographs of your best bouncy castles and inflatables. One of the best places to find these images is istockphoto.com A good picture may only cost you around £5 to £10, but you should recover your costs back almost immediately. It has been scientifically demonstrated in many marketing tests worldwide, that people are naturally more interested in a product or service if they see happy smiling people surrounding that product or service. Including these types of images on your promotional materials is another example of a Trust Factor.

32) Do not forget to have a Privacy Policy on your website. Google will give your site more trust and authority if you include a Privacy Policy. To find one, just Google it - and then adapt it to your own hire company.

33) You can also add a PayPal button (including Visa and Mastercard buttons) to your website in order to take deposits on inflatables via PayPal. This adds credibility to your website because virtually everyone is familiar with these payment symbols. (People even carry them in their wallets and purses)

34) Do not forget to also have a COOKIE POLICY page on your website - if your site stores cookies on your visitors' computers! In addition, Google will give your site extra trust and authority.

Here is an example of a Cookie Policy:

"This website uses cookies -- These are not tasty biscuits but are small text files that are placed on your computer to help the site provide a better user experience. In general, cookies are used to retain user preferences, store information for things like shopping carts, and provide anonymous tracking data to third party applications like Google Analytics. As a rule, cookies will make your browsing experience better. However, you may prefer to disable cookies on this site and on others. The most effective way to do this is to disable cookies in your browser. We suggest consulting the Help section of your browser or taking a look at the About Cookies website which offers guidance for all modern browsers."

Please also look at http://www.aboutcookies.org for more info. about cookies and your legal obligations.

35) Get a 1-minute video of you welcoming visitors to your website and watch your bookings increase. If you want to get more bookings, then it is very important to have videos on your website. This could be a video of your inflatables in action, or even better a video of some of your customers talking in front of your inflatables about how good your bouncy castles are. Video testimonials are an extremely powerful way to convince new customers to do business with you.

HOWEVER, there is another simpler way to use video, and that is to film YOURSELF talking in front of one of your best inflatables about your business, and how it can be enjoyed by your potential customers. Then upload it to YouTube. Modern smart-phones make this very easy to do. If done reasonably well (it does not have to be a Hollywood blockbuster) there are THREE big benefits to your hire business.

i. Google owns YouTube, and if it finds relevant YouTube video on your website, it will tend to rank your website higher (everything else being equal).

ii. When your potential customers see a short video of welcoming them to your website, they will feel that they 'know you a bit' and hopefully like you, BEFORE they have even picked up the phone or booked you online.
iii. If you come across as being friendly and likeable, then potential customers and clients will want to do business with you, and this may persuade them to choose your company as opposed to one of your competitors.

Part Two
70 Sure-Fire Tips For Success
In The Inflatables Hire Business

You MUST have a website
Sending photographs (or brochures if you have lots of money to spend) should grow your business and improve profits quite quickly. However, there is another way of getting photographs and brochures of your inflatables in front of potential customers much more cheaply, and considerably faster, almost instantly. I am sure you have guessed it; the solution is to have your own website on the internet.

Imagine this scenario. A potential customer calls you; after seeing your advertisement on a leaflet or the side of your van. She expresses an interest in several of your designs which you tell her about, but she is not sure which one her six year-old daughters prefer. You then tell her she can see some colour images of your inflatables on the website. She then goes away, connects to your website, shows her daughter the different designs, etc. Her daughter then chooses one and 10 minutes later is back on the phone to you to book the chosen castle. The great thing about having a website is that you do not have to spend money on photographs, brochures, envelopes, postage stamps, etc. The website does all the work for you at a fraction of the cost. Secondly, and just as importantly, your customer can view colour pictures and relevant details of your inflatables instantly, without having to wait 24 hours or more to get something in the post.

These days, any business worth its salt is expected to have a website. It really is no longer an option, but rather a necessity. Back in April 2000, I decided to have a website constructed for my own inflatable hire business. Amazingly, within 10 days of the site being up, it had already paid for itself. The website did all the selling for me! Now things have moved on, of course, as everybody has (or should have) a website. In fact, you cannot afford not to! A major additional benefit of having your own website is that it is much easier for customers to communicate with you. They can email you from your site at any time of the day or night, whichever time is convenient for them. You simply pick up your emails in the morning and then email or call them when it is convenient. If you are interested in having your own website built, please go to the resources section towards the back of this book, and we would be more than happy to help.

Build Trust and Credibility
One of the most powerful ways that you can increase your profits is to get your potential customers to **TRUST** you more - **BEFORE** they contact you to enquire or make a booking. Use the following credibility factors to attract and keep more customers.

There are many different ways of doing this; it might simply involve adding a few words or images to your website, business stationery or marketing materials such as flyers. It amazes me how few members actually take advantage of these 'TRUST FACTORS' which can have a huge positive psychological effect on your customers before they even contact you to book an inflatable!

Here is a list of what I consider to be the main 30+ 'TRUST FACTORS'.

Tip # 1 -Answer your phone
You should find a way of professionally answering all your incoming calls. If you cannot do it personally, there are businesses that exist simply to answer your phone calls. If you hit and hope with an answer phone, you will lose business.

Tip # 2 - Magnetic Business Cards
To assist you in gaining repeat business have your business cards printed on to magnetic backing. As you deliver the inflatable, you could offer to stick the card to their refrigerator.

Tip # 3 - Testimonials
Add testimonials and reviews (Use real people's names, addresses and photographs if possible - not: Mrs A from Manchester -- which looks like it is just made up and your potential customers will see straight through it!). Video testimonials from genuine happy customers are the most powerful testimonials of all!

Tip # 4 - Launch Date

Mention when you launched your company, particularly if it was some years ago. E.g. Established 1995 or "Hiring bouncy castles continually since 2002", or "delighting children continually since 2006".

Tip # 5 - Media

If you have been featured in your local newspaper or on TV mention this fact. Creates instant credibility!

Tip # 6 - Blow Your Trumpet

Mention on your website that you are a member of the BIHA do not just add the BIHA logo shield. Actually, let visitors know that you are a BIHA member! Official research has found that a whopping 94% of the general public feel more confident about contacting a company (e.g. an inflatable hire business) who is a member of a recognised industry trade body. (Source: MORI)

Tip # 7 - Smile!

Include a photograph of you and your staff or team on your website and marketing materials; it creates a more personal feel. FACT: People buy people first BEFORE they buy products or services - this is well worth remembering. Some companies have a page on their website dedicated to their team. This might include a photograph of each team member and a short bio about them. It has been proven scientifically that if you have pictures of yourself on your website and other promotional materials - then customers and prospective customers will trust you more.

Tip # 8 - Video

Include a short video of your inflatables on your website to an appealing soundtrack. Also, ensure you upload it to YouTube. This will to wow your potential customers and create a professional image. To see examples look at the videos on the BIHA homepage at **www.biha.org.uk**

Tip # 9 - Public Liability Insurance

If true, mention that you have full public liability insurance for 'peace of mind'.

Tip # 10 - Spare Capacity

If true, mention that you have spare vans and spare drivers in the event of an emergency.

Tip # 11 - Your Family
If true, mention that you have children of your own, so you realise the vital importance of reliability and punctuality.

Tip # 12 - DBS Clearance
If true, mention that you and your staff are fully DBS checked and cleared.

Tip # 13 - A Family Affair
If true, mention that you are a family-run business.

Tip # 14 - Cancellation Policy
If true, mention that there is no cancellation charge for wet or windy weather. This will further give your prospective customers peace of mind.

Tip # 15 - PIPA
If true, mention that your inflatables are PIPA registered, or RPII registered.

Tip # 16 - Search Address
Give the FULL name and address of your business. This helps customers trust you more, and also Google will tend to rank you higher in their 'Places Listing' for LOCAL searches. I am aware that some members prefer to hide their address details for fear of theft. This is understandable of course. But you need to be aware that Google may penalise your business and rank you in a lower position. This is because it does not know precisely where you are based when someone searches for a "bouncy castle in their local town".

Tip # 17 - Opening Hours
Mention your 'opening hours' for each day of the week. Many members including highly experienced hire companies forget to do this. It builds trust, and also for some reason Google seems to like it!

Tip # 18 - Contact Methods
Give your prospective customers multiple points of contact (e.g. mobile, text, email, landline, Skype, etc.) All customers have their PREFERRED method of contact which may be different from yours!

Tip # 19 - Payment Methods
If you are able to take PayPal and credit cards, then display these symbols on your website and marketing materials. These logos have been proven to

have an extremely high trust-factor when people see them. Experts on this subject even go as far as saying that when people see these logos, it actually puts them in a 'buying mood', because many people regard credit card money as not real money, but 'funny money' or 'monopoly money'. E.g. the plastic pays for it! Also, a credit card logo on your website adds professionalism to your business.

Tip # 20 - FAQ Page
Have a Frequently Asked Questions (FAQ) page. Put your customer's minds at rest by answering their most burning questions before or after they have spoken to you.

Tip # 21 - Photographs of Inflatables
Include photographs of your best inflatables, preferably above the fold (in the top section of your website, before the visitor needs to scroll down). Some members forget to include this vital trust factor.

Tip # 22 - Scarcity
Include some scarcity. For example -"In the summertime we tend to get very busy, so please book your bouncy castle early to avoid unnecessary disappointment."

Tip # 23 - Facebook and other links
Get a Facebook business page; you can also consider a Twitter, Google+1 account and Linked-In. It is important that you LINK them to your website. Google will reward you for having these and should rank your website higher up in its listings. Also, your trust factor with customers and potential customers will go through the roof! So it is worth doing!

Tip # 24 - Weather
Add a weather forecast to your website.

Tip # 25 - Year Date
Check your website has the current year at the footer and other crucial areas. Some bouncy castle hire websites I have seen have "new inflatables for" with an older year date showing. Even worse still - "new for " then again an old year date. Such a simple and obvious oversight might just prevent a potential customer from calling you. Hardly surprising as they might think your website is stale and out of date!

Tip # 26 - Blog
Add a blog to your website - Google will love it - and rank you higher - FACT!

Tip # 27 - RPII Operators Training
If you have attended an RPII Operators Training Course, then tell your prospective customers! They may not have a clue as to what it is, but the fact that you have been on a formal training course adds credibility.

Tip # 28 - Booking System
If you hire out a fairly large number and variety of inflatables, then you should seriously consider investing in an online booking system. The BIHA strongly recommend Bouncy Castle Network (**www.bouncycastlenetwork.com**).

Sometimes, a customer will be planning their child's party at 10pm (or later) when they have time after a busy day. They may feel uncomfortable about telephoning a hire company at that time. However, with an online booking system, they can book anytime they like - at their own convenience. This is a big Trust Factor!

Tip # 29 - Spelling
Check your website for spelling mistakes! This is a not a major issue, but if one of your potential customers sees a spelling mistake or two, it can appear unprofessional. They may think "Well if they cannot take care of the spelling, then what guarantee do I have that they will take care of my booking!" Perhaps this is a bit extreme, but some people are very fussy about spelling and expect people to get it right first time.

Tip # 30 - Do not Price too low
Put your prices up, or alternatively have a higher price option, e.g. an elite or super-deluxe price. If your prices are too low, especially if they are cheaper than your competitors - some potential customers may assume that your professionalism and quality of inflatables and service, etc., is less.

Tip # 31 - About Us
Have a really great "About Us" page. An About Us page is a brilliant opportunity for you to give as much information as possible to help you get more customers. Include a photograph of yourself and your team members.

Mention why you started an inflatable hire business for example. Perhaps include a short video of you welcoming visitors to your website.

Tip # 32 - Photographs of happy children having fun

Get high-quality images of happy children, (especially where they are looking directly at the camera) and put them at the top of your marketing materials and your website - alongside photographs of your best bouncy castle castles and inflatables. One of the best places to find these images is istockphoto.com.

A good pic may only cost you a small amount, yet you should make your money back almost immediately. It has been scientifically demonstrated in many marketing tests worldwide, that people are naturally more interested in a product or service if they see happy smiling people surrounding that product or service. Including these types of images on your promotional materials is another example of a Trust Factor.

Tip # 33 - Privacy Policy

Do not forget to have a Privacy Policy on your website. Google will give your site more trust and authority if you include a Privacy Policy as will your customers. To find one, just Google it - and then adapt it to your own hire company.

Tip # 34 - PayPal

You can also add a PayPal button to your website in order to take deposits on inflatables via PayPal. These can include images of Visa, Mastercard and other payment cards. This will add credibility to your website because virtually everyone is now familiar with these payment symbols.

Tip # 35 - Cookies

Do not forget to also have a COOKIE POLICY page on your website. This is not the sort you eat! Rather those stored on computers when a visitor lands on your website. In addition, Google will give your site extra trust and authority.

Tip # 36 - Welcome Video

Get a 1-minute video of you welcoming visitors to your website and watch your bookings increase! If you want to get more bookings, then it is very important to have videos on your website. This could be a video of your inflatables in action, or even better still a video of some of your customers talking in front of your inflatables about how good your bouncy castle hire business is! Video testimonials are an extremely powerful way to convince new customers to do business with you.

I do not necessarily recommend that you add all the above 'TRUST FACTORS' to your website, and other marketing material, but the more you can genuinely mention then the more will your potential customers trust you. And human nature being what it is, if they trust you, they are much more likely to book with you, even though you may not necessarily be the cheapest hire company in your area.

Traditional Marketing - Even More Tips
Over the years I have heard complaints that hirers are unable to get many bookings for their inflatables. For someone who is a brand-new startup may find they are competing directly with well-established hire companies who perhaps have flooded the area with advertising in the past. As a result, they now get the bulk of their work from repeat business and word of mouth referrals. In such a case a website or other internet marketing although good in the long term, may often not be the best solution for initial business.

Fortunately for you though, children are born every day of the week in your area, creating new and ongoing business demand. It will not go away anytime soon either. With the advent of the internet, search engines, email and websites it is all too easy to overlook what colloquially might be termed some good 'old fashioned' marketing. These should not be overlooked as they can prove to be a lucrative source of valuable inflatable bookings. With the following tips, I have tried to focus on methods that are mostly free of charge or low-cost.

Some of these ideas might seem 'old-hat' to you, whilst others will be a timely reminder of 'forgotten' marketing tips and ideas to get you more bookings throughout the entire year -not just in the peak season!

Tip # 37 - Leaflets and Flyers
Get a few thousand leaflets printed, and then contact other companies (or agencies) which do leaflet distribution, and ask for a shared leaflet drop. A

way to save money is to approach your local Pizza/Chinese/Indian takeaway, and tell them that you will deliver their leaflets for free if they pay for your printing costs! Sneaky, but it works. Get another fast-food company involved, and you could make a small profit by delivering leaflets which could contribute to your other advertising and marketing costs.

Tip # 38 - Piggybacking off Others
Contact every school, nursery, playgroup, childminder, PTA, Scout Groups, Brownie groups, Youth Clubs, After School groups, Children's Charities, Family Attraction Centres, Zoos, Farms, etc., which cater to families, in your LOCAL area. Tell them that you would be delighted to give them a FREE bouncy castle for the day or half-day (FOR FUND RAISING PURPOSES - make sure you mention this! As you may be taken a lot more SERIOUSLY by the person in charge of the group. They can hardly say no to you - if it will help raise urgently needed funds).

<u>In return for you providing a FREE bouncy castle for the day, they need to allow you to give out flyers to all the parents and children in attendance.</u>

For the lucrative corporate market, a similar version of this idea can also be effective. Contact the Social Secretary of large and Blue Chip Companies in your local area, and offer to donate a free inflatable for the day, with the idea that any funds raised will go to their chosen charity. If they jump at the chance, you can then contact your local newspaper who may well send a reporter to cover the event. All of a sudden, you have FREE newspaper advertising worth hundreds of pounds or more. A very happy charity, and hopefully a very happy company which may well use your services for future lucrative corporate events.

When I did this, I also found that I received food and other goodies throughout the course of the day. If you are too busy to attend in person, ask someone from the charity to help. They may even want to have a stand. When using this approach, adopt the mindset of FUNDRAISING, and you should be richly rewarded for your actions. In addition, you should get referrals from the parents in attendance. Also, the word may spread to other companies in your LOCAL area who are interested in hiring inflatables from you.

Tip # 39 - You scratch my back, I'll scratch yours

This can be extremely powerful. Contact other local companies in the party and events industry such as your local party shop, your local face-painter, marquee hirer, children's entertainer, event's organiser, etc. Then tell them that you would like to refer your customers over to them if they can return the favour! And also share mailings. One entrepreneurial BIHA member even helped to organise a consortium of local companies to supply the various services and equipment for the weddings in his town, via the local party/wedding shop.

Tip # 40 - Swop leads with competitors

This is a similar idea, which some may disagree with. Get to know your local competitors! Even get friendly with them! Find out what equipment they have, and do not have. For instance, they may only rent out corporate play inflatables for the adult market; in such cases, they might very well be continuously turning away people wanting children's bouncy castles, or vice versa.

Tip # 41 - Display Cards

This idea is not usually considered - even by veteran inflatable hire companies. It is extremely simple and involves taking a photograph of your best and brightest bouncy castle or another play inflatable. Then printing it out, or glueing it onto a postcard (with your contact details at the top) and then putting it up in the window of your local busy newsagents or post-offices (Costs usually only a few £'s a week).

Some supermarkets, hairdressers, fish and chip shops, etc., - let you do this for free! Virtually no-one else who advertise in shop windows does this, so your photographic advertisement will stick out like a 'sore thumb' on the newsagent's window. Do not make the common mistake of simply scribbling out an advertisement that is almost impossible to read, be professional about it.

Tip # 42 - Brand Yourself

Get some quality clothing (e.g. jackets, t-shirts, sweat-shirts, polo-jumpers, base-ball caps, etc.) and then get your company logo and contact details printed on them. I have known situations where a BIHA member has been in a queue to pay for diesel, and someone behind them has tapped them on the shoulder, and told them that they want to hire a bouncy castle from them, just because their name and logo was on the back of their jacket :-) Very powerful, and means waiting in a queue with lots of people around you can actually be profitable -and it is free. Which brings us to our next tip.

Tip # 43 - Always carry your business cards and flyers with you!
You never know who you will meet while you are out and about! There are some instances where a local public centre (e.g. your local library, community centre, vets, doctor's surgery, etc.) will allow you to place your flyers free of charge.

Tip # 44 - Infomercials
Local newspapers are frequently interested in featuring local business people and their accomplishments. This is free advertising and should always be used. You can also contact your local community magazine and offer to write a monthly or weekly guest column for them, and include your author bio and website address.

Tip # 45 - Ask for Referrals
It pretty much goes without saying that every time that you make a booking, you should be asking the customer for referrals. If you feel uncomfortable asking them directly, then you can do it indirectly. For example, giving them vouchers to give to their friends, relatives and neighbours. I have even heard of BIHA members who will pay a small commission to their customers if they refer them to new customers such as: "Get a free bouncy castle for every 10 people that you refer to us".

Tip # 46 - Contact Local Companies
Write to the social secretary or HR Department of local businesses and make them aware of your services. Even better make an appointment to go round to see them. Many medium to large companies have family fun days in the summer, team-building events and other corporate events throughout the year.

Tip # 47 - Local Involvement
Get involved in your LOCAL community. Look for groups and associations that align with your priorities and values, such as your local Chamber of Commerce. Volunteerism is a great way to network as well. I

knew a chap who connected with the local Asian community in his town. He did a good job, and within weeks had more than enough work to keep him busy during the season.

Tip # 48 - Signage
Get a magnetic sign made for your car as well as your business vehicle. For the one-time cost of the sign, your business name will be on display everywhere you drive. Do not cut people up though and no road rage, please! A lot of hire companies have gorgeous sign-written vans, but they overlook the obvious - to advertise their hire business on the side and/or back of their car!

Tip # 49 - Reviews
Write good reviews for local businesses and send them off to them by or email. Local businesses love positive reviews, and the more they have on the internet and in their brochures and flyers the better. So help out your local businesses by being a good customer, then getting online and writing about your experiences. You will gain favour from your fellow business owners and potential customers who are researching local businesses. They will keep seeing your name pop up and, of course, the name of your inflatable hire business.

Tip # 50 - Newsletters
Start a FREE monthly (or quarterly) newsletter to all your customers and people who express an interest in your hire services. If you send out such via email, it will also end up costing you nothing but a little time.

Tip # 51 - Affiliates
You can use 'affiliates' to help you get more bookings. There are plenty of 'stay at home mums (or dads)', students, retired people, etc. They would be more than happy to get bookings for you using some of the above methods in return for a commission on each hire.

Dealing with Customers

Tip # 52 - First Impressions Count
It always amazes me how unprofessional some small companies can be when they answer the telephone to a prospective customer. Unfortunately,

this also applies to some inflatable hire companies. In the mind of a customer, their first impressions and initial opinions of a company they are thinking of dealing with are made in the first 5 seconds of the phone call. When my van needed a repair recently, the greetings I got from repairers when I rang them up ranged from "Yep Steve here" to "Good Morning XYZ Van Repairs -David speaking, how can I help". I felt more at ease with David than I did with Steve, purely because his greeting was friendlier and professional. David eventually got my business. When you answer the phone to customers be friendly, positive and professional. Enthusiasm also helps.

When I first started hiring inflatables way back in 1991, I made the following mistake. A potential customer would ring me up and ask me about prices, etc. I would then look at my price list and would tell the caller "parrot" fashion how much each size would cost. Not surprisingly, the caller would usually say something like - "I may get back to you", or "I'll think about it". After a few months, I realised that I was doing something seriously wrong, so I completely changed my approach. Instead of reeling off a load of prices and hoping for the best I would ask the customer several questions such as -"How old are the children", "How many are you expecting", "Are you having the party indoors or outdoors," etc. In other words, I was pro-active as opposed to being reactive which can make all the difference. When they give me the answers, I will then recommend a particular size of unit.

This approach always results in more bookings as a ratio to enquiries. The reason for this is because the customer feels you are taking an interest in their children and the party, and more importantly, you are developing a rapport with the customer. It is an established fact in sales that people buy people first. This means that before someone books an inflatable with yourself, (particularly a new customer) they have to like you and trust you first. The only way you can achieve this is by having a pro-active approach and seeing things from your customer's point of view. This is largely achieved by asking the caller leading questions. I cannot overemphasise the importance of this. You will get a lot more bookings if you follow this approach.

Tip # 53 - The Provisional Pencil

Sometimes when I have gone through the standard questions which I normally ask when getting an enquiry for an inflatable, I get the following response: "I need to speak to my husband before I book anything", or "I need to speak to my work colleagues first". This reaction always slightly amuses me because most customers (you would have thought) would speak to their husband or work colleagues before making the initial phone call. I have a theory that the reason they say this is because there are still one or two doubts in their mind, whether or not they want to book with you or not, or that they are reluctant to pay the price which you have quoted.

To get around this problem, I would sometimes say to the customer, "Would you like me to provisionally pencil your booking in the diary? Then if your husband agrees to it, I can turn it into a confirmed booking. If on the other hand, he does not agree, ring me up tomorrow, and I will cancel this provisional booking -no obligation". The psychological magic words are 'provisionally pencil', it works 70% of the time, they then agree to this and rarely cancel afterwards. It is similar to a risk-free guarantee in that you are taking the risk upon their behalf. Use it, it works!

Tip # 54 - Find out price points

Occasionally, I when I have given a hire price to a potential customer, they might reply by saying "That it is too much, or too expensive". When they say this, I could just say, "Okay thanks for calling, goodbye". However, I do not and you should not either. It is like a Rolls Royce dealer because you need a car. The likelihood is for most people it is way too expensive, but a basic hatchback might be just the right price. With that in mind find out what the customer's price points are. How much too much?? £1, £5, £10, £20? I always try and find out, so that I can possibly hire them a smaller and cheaper inflatable.

Tip # 55 - Deluxe Castle Approach

Aligned with what has just been said above it is a very good idea to use the deluxe approach to getting more business. Not everyone wants a cheap bouncy castle. When a customer phones to book an inflatable, you have no real idea whether they are a multi-millionaire or on income support, or somewhere in-between. With the deluxe approach, you can target the customer in relation to how much they want to spend on their inflatable, in a particularly subtle way. This approach works as follows: If a customer rings for a quote for say a 12 x 12 castle, you say to them: " Would you like the economy, standard or deluxe castle". They will then usually say what do you mean? You tell them that the economy unit is 3 years old. The standard units are 1 -2 years old, (and are so many pounds more) and the deluxe units are under 1 year old (and even more extra pounds).

Customers with a high disposable income will tend to book deluxe and standard units, whilst less well-off customers will book the economy units. However, do remember that this is not always the case; children love inflatables so much that their parents will often make a big financial sacrifice to hire 2 or 3 inflatables for their child's birthday party. When using the deluxe approach to increase profits, you can use any combination of variables, not necessarily just based on the age or condition of the inflatable. For example, you could say that with the deluxe service, they get the inflatable delivered the day before the party; with the standard service, it is the morning of the party, and with the economy service it is up to an hour before the party starts. Use your imagination with this deluxe approach; there are many different variations which you can try until you find the one which you are most comfortable with.

Tip # 56 - Using Photographs
About 6 years ago, I came up with a very simple idea which virtually doubled the size of my business, and the number of my customers increased beyond all expectations. For some time I had considered going to my local printers and getting some colour glossy brochures printed up to send to customers wanting more information. At the time the cost of doing this would have been at least £1000 + VAT. That was for only 250 brochures. Far more than I could afford at the time.

Another problem was if I bought any new inflatables at a later date, they would not be in the brochure. However, it suddenly occurred to me that a much less expensive alternative to brochures was to take some colour photographs of my inflatables, then get a large number of reprints. I would then send these off to prospective customers, with a covering letter and price list. Now interestingly the cost of getting 1000 photographs developed was just under a £100 at the time. A massive saving of over £900! However, to my surprise, there was an additional benefit which outweighed even the cost savings. I found out about this new benefit as a result of positive feedback from customers. I will try and explain this benefit as clearly as possible.

When a customer receives a glossy colour brochure, they may be really impressed and love the colour images. However, the problem with a brochure is that it is impersonal, and many people just have a browse through, and then put it away for safe keeping. I am convinced that many people have been conditioned to admire the quality of a good brochure, but a relatively few number of people actually buy just from a brochure. On the other hand, a photograph or set of photographs sent to a prospective customer is breathtakingly personal. I have actually had customers phone me the day they received my photographs, expressing their gratitude, and commenting on the good service. Some customers even think that I took the photographs specifically for them and went on to book their inflatable immediately.

Another reason, why more bookings usually result from photographs as opposed to brochures, is because when people receive photographs in the post, e.g. from friends, it is usually of exciting events such as holidays and marriages. Importantly, these photographs always get shown around the family, relatives and the neighbours. So there is built-in psychology going on there. So when you send your photographs to your customers, the same kind of thing can happen, albeit on a smaller scale. When I send photographs out to customers, I always make sure that my company name and telephone number are on the back as well as the size of the inflatable on the photograph.

Try and use a good quality camera; you will get even more bookings if the print quality is excellent. If a potential customer rang me and did not book an inflatable there and then, I would often ask them if they would be interested in receiving some photographs and an information pack. Around 9 times out of 10, they say yes, and of the people who received those photographs - 60% -75% would book. One other advantage in doing this is that you now have a potential customers' name and address -so that you can write to them again. A useful way of reducing your costs still further is to photocopy some of your photographs, and then you can send a mixture of colour photographs and black and white photocopies. Try and send colour photographs of your best inflatables. Things have moved on since I personally done this. High-resolution photographs can often be taken on a mere smartphone, and digital printing costs are now very competitive.

Tip # 57 - Using Customers to promote
Every time I hire out an inflatable, I always hand out a dozen or so A5 or A6 sized leaflets, with my phone number on for the customer to hand out to their guests. As mentioned elsewhere you should really always have these to hand. These leaflets are just photocopies and usually work very well, they are cheap to produce. I usually get at least one booking for every batch of leaflets which I give out at a party.

Tip # 58 - Team up with others
An excellent idea of getting more business is to team up with other companies which are in a similar business. Examples are children's entertainers, magicians, and companies which provide party related items, e.g. barbeques and wedding equipment. If you already have a reciprocal agreement with these companies, they refer business to you and in return for which you pass business onto them. The secret to making this idea work well is to develop good working relationships between the different companies.

It is then relatively easy to boost your profits by hiring out add-on support products, at the same time that you set up the inflatable at the customers' premises. Examples of add-on support products are helium balloons, mini-marquees, party bags, and tables and chairs. Thinking bigger you can team to provide face-painting all the way to food and drink stalls.

Tip # 59 - The Dennis Emery Profit System
This superb idea is, in a nutshell, as follows. Many children's parties have a theme to them, e.g. pirates, barbie doll, mermaids, animals, etc. Imagine if you could supply your customers with a themed bouncy castle of their choice to match as closely as possible the theme of the party or the birthday child's favourite character. How much extra would your customers be prepared to pay to have the theme of their choice? £5, £10 or even £15? How many extra referrals would you get? Traditionally, the only way to do this was to go to the huge expense of buying a themed bouncy castle. However, the big disadvantage of doing this is that the theme may

go out of fashion with children and you are then stuck with a castle which no-one wants to hire.

The ingenious solution to this problem is to have detachable artwork panels which have Velcro attached to them, and so can be interchanged between different bouncy castles, to suit the relevant theme of the party. Each artwork panel is made from bouncy castle material and is approx. 5ft high and 3 ft wide. They fit snugly around the two front pillars of the castle. The castle also has to have Velcro glued to the front pillars, in order for the artwork to be securely attached. I used to use heavy duty duct tape, to secure the 2 artwork panels. However, I found that this left a messy residue, and also in wet weather, it would come off. If you are interested in buying some detachable artwork panels of the theme of your choice, including the all-important

Velcro strips, look in the resources section towards the back of this book. It will put you in touch with the companies which produces the artwork, the panels and the Velcro at very reasonable prices. The artwork on these Velcro panels must NOT infringe upon anyone's intellectual property rights.

Tip # 60 - Free Castle for Leaflet Promotion
This next idea is astonishing in its simplicity but can generate a huge amount of extra business. This involves writing to a few local playgroups, nurseries and schools and telling them that they can have a FREE bouncy castle or ball pond for the day if they promise to hand out your leaflets and give you some well-deserved free publicity. The mums will see your inflatable and providing it is clean, and in good condition, you should get quite a lot of referrals from it. Similarly, if you supply free of charge an inflatable for your local shopping centre, if its busy, you will get bookings and referrals from it. It certainly helps to have your phone number painted on the front of the unit, and you should always give lots of leaflets out. There is another angle to this as well. The fact you are providing the castle for free reflects well in the local community. This, in turn, means you will be considered first when a mum needs a bouncy castle for her child. She would have met you personally, and her child would have already enjoyed your generosity.

Tip # 61 - Emergency Call Out Service

This works very well if you are very well organised in the running of your business. It involves running an <u>Emergency Call Out Service</u>. It is a well-known fact that at the beginning of each summer, several 'Cowboy' bouncy castle hire companies set up in all the major towns with the intention of making a quick buck, during the peak season and then selling up in the winter. What separates them from established hirers, is that they rarely have P/L insurance, they often operate with worn-out and dirty inflatables, and perhaps most serious of all is that they sometimes forget (or just do not care) to deliver the castle to the customer. One summer, I had about 50 calls from frantic people telling me that they had been let down as the castle had not arrived and the party was starting in 10 minutes! Because of the short notice involved, and also because it was often in the next town, I was rarely able to help. This concerned me deeply because I felt that it would harm the entire reputation of the inflatable hire industry. 'Cowboy' or 'Fly by Night' companies all too often only have one or two units, therefore in the busy summer period, they get double booked with alarming frequency. Not that they care of course. But you can take advantage of this situation if you so wish. When you advertise your inflatables for hire, have the words "Emergency Call Out Service Available". Also, write it on your flyers which you hand out at parties. A word of warning though - word will get around that you can provide an emergency call out service to customers who have been let down by 'Cowboy' companies. Then you are likely to get very busy during the summer months when the demand for inflatables far exceeds the supply. Make sure you have sufficient inflatables, transport and the organisational ability to cope. Your emergency call out service will also get known by other hirers in the area, who may pass business onto you at the last minute. One summer, another inflatable hirer operating in the same town as me, found to his dismay that his back axle had broken, halfway through his deliveries at 10am on a Saturday morning. To make matters worse his spare van was being serviced. He was able to call a few other hirers and me to help him finish his deliveries. Again this is another area that could prove lucrative. But only if you have the capacity, organisation and ability to deal with the inevitable stress caused to all when dealing with such emergencies.

Tip # 62 - Working Relationships

This idea follows on from the last idea. The BIHA strongly recommend that inflatable hirers operating in the same town or vicinity should develop close working relationships. If this is achieved, it means that leads can be shared out, especially if one hirer is fully booked. They can then pass on leads and bookings to another reputable hirer, who is perhaps not so busy. I have come across hirers in some towns who will not pass the time of day if they bump into another hirer. I have also known of cases where the rivalry between hirers in a town has been so intense, that rather than pass a booking to a competitor, a hirer has instead chosen to let down a prospective customer, even where they have known where a castle is available for hire. This is a very unprofessional and selfish business practice, and it is not recommended. An important aim of the BIHA is to try and bring inflatable hirers together who are perhaps working in the same town. We believe that if leads are passed around, everyone will benefit, and every reputable company will become more profitable over the years.

Tip #63 - Magnetic Sign Business Vehicle

A very good way of promoting your business completely for free is to stick a magnetic sign on the sides and back of your van, or estate car, with the name of your company and the telephone company.

Tip #64 -Accessories and 'Add-on hire products'

This excellent idea which expands on another tip, but uses a slightly different approach. It concerns the use of accessories to complement your bouncy castle bookings. Every time a customer books an inflatable, you have a golden opportunity whilst they are on the phone (after they have booked!) to make additional money for very little extra work. Examples of accessories which you can offer your customers to make extra profits are - balloons, including helium balloons; face-painting, party-bags, mini-marquees, tables and chairs, crockery, magician service, children's entertainer, trampolines, toy trains for children to ride on, quality toys to hire at parties, etc. There are probably a lot more examples of accessories. Give customers a choice as to what they would like to hire in addition to the inflatable. If they cannot decide at the point they book the inflatable, ring them back a day or two later. If you provide a good service for your accessories, you will also get a lot more referrals. It is strongly recommended that you firstly do some research to see what are the most popular types of accessories in your area. Also, have a look at the competition. Perhaps you can strike up a deal with a competitor, such that they give you bouncy castle bookings, and in return for which, you give them bookings for their 'accessories'. Spend some time doing some research, and ask your existing customers what they would be most interested in to hire, or buy to run alongside your inflatable.

Tip #65 - Raffle Tickets for payment
This next idea is a very clever concept recently passed to us from an existing BIHA member. It addresses a very real problem when supplying a large inflatable to a public event. Traditionally, the inflatable is sited, and children (and adults!) pay anything from 50p to £2 to have a go. At the end of the event, the operator usually gives a percentage of the takings to the organisers of the event or a designated charity. Alternatively, the operator will be asked for a pitch fee , (e.g. at a car boot sale or a school fete) of at least £20. We have heard about hirers who have been asked for as much as £500 per day to site their inflatables at airshows. If the weather is favourable, and the public (and their children!) turn up in their droves, it can be very profitable indeed. However, unfortunately, this system is open to abuse and dishonesty by the person taking the money. Firstly, the operator may employ someone to take the money off the public.
If you the operator are not present, how do you know for example, that the takings were only £750? They may have been £1000, but your employee dishonestly pocketed £250 of the takings. How can you make sure that you are not being ripped off, even though you are not present? Easy, when you know! You buy a big book of raffle tickets, and you instruct your employee to hand a raffle ticket to every person that has a go on the inflatable. If they have more than one go, they get more than one ticket. At the end of the event, you draw a raffle ticket out of a hat, and the winner gets a quality prize which you bought beforehand. By handing out raffle tickets, there are several benefits. Firstly, more people are likely to want to go the inflatable in the first place, as there is a prize at the end. Secondly, you can keep tags as to who has been on the inflatable and who has not. Thirdly, and the biggest benefit of all is that you will know exactly how many raffle tickets have been given out because every single ticket has a

duplicate in the book. If your employee tries to fiddle you out of a few pounds, this will show up as the duplicate raffle tickets and will not reconcile with the monies taken. It is important to make it known to customers at the outset that they will get free entry into the raffle, every time that they have a go of the inflatable. If it is a good prize, you will make a lot more profits as well.

Tip #66 - Preventing Adults using inflatables
We have all suspected it and even seen adults abusing bouncy castles designed for children. This is despite informing them during installation that doing such could cause damage to the bed seams and the stress points (e.g. where the pillars meet the bed). I remember turning up to pick up a bouncy castle to be confronted by several extremely heavy adults pounding away as if their lives depending on it. Yes, it did sustain damage as a result.

Though slightly controversial, the following idea will often prevent such abuse. It involves painting in large clear letters on the back wall of the castle. "NOT TO BE USED BY ADULTS". If an adult jumps on to have a bounce, the children will often shout at the adult to get off, purely because of the notice. Contrary to popular belief children do not mind such signs. In their eyes it simply confirms the castle being the children's domain not there's. In addition, it is one thing for a parent to disregard your instructions. It is quite another to blatantly break a rule in front of their own children.

Tip #67 - Reducing wear on the bed seams of the inflatable
There are several ways of making your bed seams stronger and less susceptible to wear. The best method is to get them webbed with a material very similar to car seatbelts. Another way of reducing wear on the seams is to put a slightly more powerful blower than you would normally use. I have personally used a 1.5hp blower instead of a 0.75hp blower. I also find that the castle is a lot bouncier, and the children enjoy it a lot more. Talking of blowers ...

Tip #68 - How to increase the power of your electric fans by up to 25%
This only takes about 5 minutes per fan and does not involve dismantling the fan or undertaking any electrical work. During normal use, whilst the

impeller in the fan is spinning at high RPM, it builds up a strong static charge which has the unfortunate effect of picking up dust and dirt, insects and other debris and depositing it on the actual blades of the impeller as if stuck by 'glue'. This gradual build-up of debris reduces the efficiency of the impeller in the same way that the build-up of ice on an aircraft's wing can reduce its aerodynamic lifting ability. When the impellors blades have become really clogged up over say an entire season, then the amount of air being blown out into the inflatable can be reduced by as much as 25%. This can mean that the inflatable is only partially inflated, which rapidly increases the wear on the unit, and causes a safety hazard.

In order to remove this debris from the impeller blades I normally use a long thin metal tent peg, which I insert at the funnel end and then carefully clean the impellor getting as much of the debris off as possible. The removed debris will fall back into the blades, but when you switch the blower on, all the loose debris will shoot out, so be very careful of your eyes. After you have cleaned the impeller blades, you will notice an improvement in the force of air coming out.

Tip #69 - Prevent rain-water being sucked into the inflatable

Very simple, place a plastic picnic table (approx. 4ft in diameter) over the blower. You can remove 2 legs of the table to create a steep slope for the water to run down. Incredibly simple, but in heavy rain, it can save you a lot of time and effort at roll-up time.

Tip #70 - Getting paid when it rains

A very simple idea to make sure that you still get paid, even if the weather has been extremely wet and the castle has hardly been used. If the weather is exceptionally bad and as a result, the castle does not get used. Then promise the customer that they can have the castle again on a dryer day, and only pay say £5, which should pay the fuel at least. I always used to give the customer the opportunity to cancel before delivery anyhow, if the weather forecast was very grim. I did not charge a cancellation fee in such cases. However being out of pocket after the effort of delivery and pickup is quite another thing. At least this way you effectively get 50% of the hire costs as opposed to none. Also from the customer's point of view, you have met them halfway. Better still how about an idea to overcome the bad weather problem altogether.

Tip #71 - Beating bad weather
One of the biggest problems with hiring bouncy castles in the UK, of course, is the unpredictable weather. Short of moving your entire business to Spain (now there's a thought) we just have to get on with it. One day it can be glorious sunshine, and your phone does not stop ringing. The next day it can be torrential rain. Heavy rain causes all sorts of problems for hirers. When the bouncy castle gets very wet the children's enjoyment is reduced and often, especially if it has hardly been used, the customer expects a discount or even a refund. Most bouncy castles have rain-covers or shower covers, but in prolonged heavy rain these tend to be inadequate.

How many times have you collected a castle after a very wet day, to find that not only is the rain cover soaking wet, but so too is the inflatable? It then becomes a nightmare to try and get as much water off it as possible (both inside and outside), and then to try and roll it up while it is still soaking wet. Yuk! Perhaps the biggest problem of all is trying to lift a soaking wet bouncy castle which weighs half a ton onto your sack trolley. Then you have to get it into your van when it can be nearly double the normal weight, because of all the rainwater inside.

Well, fortunately, there is a unique solution which goes a long way toward solving this problem of wet weather. It has been tried and tested, so it is proven to work. Admittedly it takes a little time and effort -but you are rewarded when the roll-up time comes around!

We will now look at this solution step-by-step.

Step 1
In very wet weather rainwater gets sucked into the electric or petrol fan, and then gets forced deep inside the castle, adding enormously to the weight of the unit when it is rolled up, and coming up through the bed seams, when the castle is being used, and causing bubbles and froth. To prevent this rainwater being sucked into the blower, buy a plastic picnic table (approx. 4ft diameter) from any good DIY shop. If you then place this table over the fan, when it is raining, it will stop water from coming in the side vent, but still allow the fan to suck air in.

Step 2
You will also need a heavy-duty rain cover, that is oversized. For my 12ft x 12ft castles I used a large piece of heavy duty tarpaulin (similar to what market traders use as a roof on their stalls) that measured about 25ft x 25ft. I then lay this cover over the deflated castle. Then using a helper, or even the customer to hold one side of the cover, whilst I held the other side. The fan is then switched on and as the castle inflates Ensure that the rain cover is evenly distributed over the castle.

Step 3
Once the castle is fully inflated use string or twine to tie the rain cover to the metal stakes at each corner. The cover has eyelets spaced at intervals all the way around. As the rain cover is so oversized, it should seal up any gaps at the sides and back of the inflatable. In case of windy weather, you may need an extra person to help hold the rain cover in place prior to it being tied down.

Step 4
At this stage, the rain cover should be securely attached to the castle, with no gaps showing. The front of the rain cover should be hanging loosely downwards, obscuring the bed of the castle. At this point get two telescopic keep net poles which can be bought from your local fishing tackle shop. Then press the sharp bit into the ground, about 7 feet in front of the castle and to the left. Repeat this procedure with the other pole, but this time put it 7 feet out from the castle, but on the opposite side to the right.

Step 5
Now take hold of the front of the rain cover, which is hanging downwards in a vertical position and move it outwards. It should be at about 45 degrees such that it forms an awning, which protrudes about 8 feet from the front of the castle. You then need to tie this 'awning' to the two keep net poles. Because the keep net poles are adjustable, you can alter the angle of the awning. I recommend a very steep angle in very heavy rain. Providing

everything is securely tied, the children should be 99% dry when using the castle.

IMPORTANT: Always make sure that any exposed electrics, e.g. plug sockets are fully protected by a waterproof bag, or better still, that you use waterproof connectors.

Bouncy Castles Disasters and Lessons To Be Learned From Them!

Below I have chronicled 70 true-life Bouncy Castle 'Horror' stories. (Including 'hirings from hell). They are bouncy castle hire bookings which went wrong, sometimes disastrously -but often with hilarious consequences (and some important lessons to be learnt -especially concerning safety and the importance of improving customer service). Some of these are stories from my own business experience. Others have been contributed by other BIHA members -enjoy!

1. We delivered a castle to a house on a big estate, late one morning. The garden was only just wide enough for this particular castle so having squeezed it through the side gate into the garden we realised things were going to be tight in the garden, too. The father was the only one there at the time, so he was watching. He sorted out the electric point for us while we started to lay out the ground sheet. Suddenly we realised that there was, on closer inspection, a fair amount of dog poo on the lawn, so we asked the man if he could remove it while we carried the rest of the equipment through to the back of the house. While we were doing this, we watched him pick up a pair of tongs off the barbecue that was out in the garden, obviously going to be used that afternoon, and proceed to pick up or flick the dog poo off to the edge of the garden. We could not believe what we were seeing, so quickly finished putting up the castle and left. On the way home, we jokingly said that he surely would not use those tongs to cook with! Surely he would not?

    Well, when we went back later to pick up the castle guess what he was using to cook with?

    Yes, I am afraid that it was the very same tongs with which he had cooked; believe it or not, he was cooking sausages!

    We collected our equipment and got out of there as quickly as possible before we were offered a sausage, as often our customers did offer us a drink or something to eat as a friendly gesture.

I promise this is a true story and is just one of many situations that we have encountered.

2. I did a hire for the girl guides for a fun day in October 2004. I delivered one of my new 15ft x 15ft castles with a shower cover in case of rain that day.

On the day it did rain, so the event was moved indoors, but the castle had to stay *out* because of the ceiling size. They hired it from 1pm - 4p.m. It was up and running by 12.45p.m when I left, expecting to return about 3.45pm.

I got back to the unit at around 3.15pm to collect another castle and was told they wanted early uplift because of poor attendance. As I arrived to pick up the castle, there were loads of children playing football in the rain. To my horror they were using my castle as the goals, one was even on it with his football boots on. I went ballistic, grabbed the kid with the boots on and ordered him off the castle, which by now was covered in mud and torn on the base.

I went into the centre to confront the hirer only to be told they had left one hour beforehand.

After many phone calls to the hirer, I got through to her mother. The girl who had hired the castle looked about 19yrs old but turned out to be only 15. The guides refused any compensation saying the girl was acting on her own and not with their permission.

I was left well out of pocket by the whole thing, and the last straw was that the police reported me to the P F for assault on a 15 year-old boy. WHAT A DAY THAT WAS. *P.S. The P F said there was no case to answer because no one saw me throw him off the castle, other than my co-worker - who does not see very well though.*

3. The following true story took place at a school fete during the long, hot summer of 2003. A child suffered a minor injury on a large children's slide (a bruise on the thigh). Unfortunately, one of the teachers panicked and dialled '999'. By pure coincidence, there was a paramedic helicopter flying past. The helicopter pilot was radioed by the ambulance service and made an emergency landing next to the slide. Unfortunately, the powerful rotor-wash from the whirring blades of the helicopter (as it landed), almost blew the slide over (while there were children still on it). It was only due to the fact that it was well staked down that a potential tragedy was avoided. Furthermore, several gazebos were blown away and destroyed.

This story was mentioned in the local press.

Moral: Always ensure your slides are well staked down. It could be a calm day, but you never know if a helicopter could tip it!

4. A booking we had last year was in the grounds of a village hall. After we had left, the customer decided she wanted it *inside*. Instead of contacting us, she and her friend removed all the anchor stakes, dragged the entire castle without rolling it or folding it, and dragged it through a single width door still with the blower attached!

We arrived to find a castle with the inflation tube twisted, the castle soft because the airflow was restricted, and absolutely no anchor points secured at all on a slippery polished wooden floor! (We would have secured it with sandbags if we had been notified).

When questioned about the safety issue, and of course the possibility of damage to our equipment, the hirer just did not care - she even had the impertinence to complain about the bed being soft, which was caused by the twisted inflation tube!

That day our own personal 'blacklist' was born!

5. One member supplied a bouncy castle to a village hall which had a hard wooden floor. After setting the castle up, he put a large safety mat at the front and said his goodbyes to the customer. Just as he was leaving, another chap (not a BIHA member) turned up with another castle. He did not have any safety mats so he 'borrowed' without permission the crash mat from the first castle and put it in front of his castle (outrageous behaviour)!

6. We had to deliver our 16ft x 16ft castle to a customer to whom we had delivered the previous year. Although we had delivered to this area before it was the same castle on both occasions. The customer gave me her address, thinking I knew where it was I did not feel the need to look it up. She also said she had to take her daughter dancing on that morning, but she would leave the side gate open for us.

7. We arrived at the house and knocked on the door; there was no answer, so I said to my helper, "No problem she is leaving the gate open for us." We went into the back garden, cussed a bit because she had not moved the swing and garden ornaments as she had promised, but I continued to move them anyway. The castle was rolled out, electrics and mats put in place and we waited for her to return. As we were very busy had a lot on that day, and we had now waited for about 15 minutes, I decided to leave her a note advising her just to plug it in. I then went to the car (which was parked in a lay-by, because we could not get the car and trailer up the little lane) to get some note paper. I thought I would try phoning the customer in case she was at home and had not heard the door. To my surprise, she answered, and I explained that we had knocked and had gone into the back garden to set up. She apologised and said she would come out to us. A few minutes went by, and the phone rang, the customer said, "I am in my back garden, and you're not here" - it was then that I asked her to clarify the address. To our horror, we were at the wrong house. It was worse because we had reorganised this garden taking out a swing and a water feature, we had also moved plant pots and toys. We have never packed a castle away so quickly! After loading everything into the trailer, the customer pulled up alongside our car on her way to

fetch her daughter from dancing. We then had to talk our way out of a very embarrassing situation.

We did contact the other householder whose garden we had trashed, who had been on holiday at the time. Since I am female and blonde, I do not need to explain what my husband said!

8. I have had a few difficult customers, but none like these. I do not send out confirmation letters. I have only had two double bookings. One was with another company I swap bookings with. His answer to my question, "What are you doing here Dave?" was, "I will give you three guesses?" I left and let him argue the toss. He managed to get some petrol money, but that was it. I rang him later and offered to split the money or pass him another booking. We operate in different areas but overlap a bit as he is in the next Town. Our business relationship is better than any one customer.

I only accept cash on delivery. That is always the last thing we tell them. I get people asking to pay when I collect, or can I give you a cheque. No Money, No Castle. I have heard all the excuses. Below is a list of the Hard Luck Stories and my replies.

Customer: "I haven't had my giro yet."
Hirer: "I need the money to feed my kids this week. Otherwise, I would give it to you for free."
Customer: "Oh."
Customer: "I don't have any cash in the house."
Hirer: "No Worries, I got a few more castles to deliver. I will be back in about 2 hours, plenty of time to get to the cash-point."
Customer: "I will see if my husband, etc., has any cash."
Customer: "Oh isn't that lucky, he had just enough in his wallet."
Hirer: "Thanks love, see you later."
Customer: "There is your £40 mate."
Hirer: "Sorry it is £ 50 mate."
Customer: "But the guy on the phone said it was £ 40."

Hirer: "I was the guy on the phone. It's £50 if that's too much I can take it away."

Customer: "Oh right, my mistake."

I may seem hard, but I have been in business before. If someone can take a liberty, they will. I do not raise my voice, and I try to be polite.

I have a slight twist on the customer is always right. The customer is always right when they are making me money; if they are costing me money, they are wrong. I do make mistakes, should I be a bit late I will ring and tell them as soon as possible and knock off £5 for their inconvenience, only had to do it once so far. I hate big posh houses (Mostly tight and treat you like the 'hired staff'.) I love council estates. (Nearly always have the cash ready. Offer you a brew and do not look down on you.)

9. I did a boot sale on Sunday with a 10ft slide and made the grand total of £12 after paying for the pitch. It is just not worth it; I should have stayed home and watched the golf. One funny point was as I let it down an old lady came up to me and said, "How much?" I said, "£1." She said, "How will I get it home?"

10. A hire company received a phone call saying that a group of travellers had parked their vehicles and caravans, etc., on a wide lay-by of a busy dual carriageway. As there were children in the group, they needed entertainment (i.e. a bouncy castle and other inflatables). The hire company was asked if they could rent out this equipment and petrol blowers for the day.

Unfortunately, the hire company agreed and delivered and set-up the inflatables on the lay-by powered by the petrol blowers.

At an agreed time, towards the end of the day, the hire company went to collect their kit and to their shock found that the lay-by was completely empty. Not only had the customer and their friends disappeared, but had also taken the inflatables with them.

This booking should never have happened, as the risk of theft was just too high from the outset.

11. Recently, a BIHA member was driving his Transit-sized van down a very quiet residential street in Reading looking for his customer's house so that he could deliver a bouncy castle. Some of the house numbers were difficult to read, and as a result, the member slowed down in his van to get a better look. However, just at that moment a police motor-cyclist pulled him over and gave him a £30 fine for slowing down and causing an obstruction on a public highway. There followed a massive row between the member and the police-officer as the member pointed out that he was making a delivery and had to slow down in order to find the customer's house. In response to this, the officer said that the driver should park his van at the top of the road and then walk down looking for the house. The driver said this was ridiculous and unnecessary bearing in mind it was a very quiet street. The driver refused to pay the fine and has made an official complaint to the Police Complaints Authority, to investigate.

12. One operator hit a stake in the ground, and it punctured a gas pipe. This incident should never have happened.

    Metal stakes (anchor points) need to be a minimum of 380mm long and 16mm thick. If you hit them in at 45 degrees they only travel 12 inches deep into the ground (300mm) - All services should be deeper than this. If you think your equipment need longer stakes to be secure - what it needs is more anchor points and stakes. I consider an anchor point every 8-10 feet to be appropriate.

13. One Thursday we went to a house to deliver a 3-month old 15ft x15ft castle. We were greeted by the tenant at the back door and asked to take it around the back where he had set up an extension lead, birthday banners, balloons, etc., ready for his child's party. All went well; the paperwork signed, deposit given, we arranged a collection time of 8pm, all was great until we arrived to collect the castle! Knocked on the front door, no reply. Went around to the back, the

castle had GONE along with mats, fan, stakes, the whole lot had been STOLEN, and the house was completely empty. Neighbours who had seen us deliver to the address THEN decided to tell us that the house had been empty for a few months and they found it strange that we were delivering to the house in the first place. Apparently, the man who took delivery of my castle was the previous tenant and was still using his old key to obtain entrance to the property. We are not sure how we could have prevented this theft, but I guess one lives and learns, and pray to God that the insurance company pays out (fingers crossed).

14. One member provided a large bouncy castle for a school fun day. One of the other attractions was for a massive army Chinook helicopter to fly into the school playing field, and land in one corner well away from all of the other attractions. As a precautionary measure, the member deflated the bouncy castle and waited for the helicopter to take off. Unfortunately, as the Chinook took off, even though it was over 50 yards from the deflated castle, the incredible power from the exhaust of its jet engines somehow got underneath the castle and tried to lift it upwards. The castle was fully staked down, and when the anchor points reached their limit, there was suddenly a huge split in the fabric. The castle could not be used for the rest of the day, and some rather colourful words were passed on to the pilot.

15. During the summer of 2005, there were some troubles in the centre of Belfast in Northern Ireland. They were so serious that they were headline news on TV. During these troubles, a BIHA member delivered a brand new 12ft x 12ft bouncy castle to a front garden in a house in Belfast, which, unfortunately, was right in the middle of the trouble. At the end of the day's hire, the member was supposed to go back to the house to collect the castle. However, due to the violence, the police had put up road-blocks, and the member decided to collect the castle once the trouble had died down. He was very concerned as a bouncy castle in the middle of a 'war-zone' is not to be recommended.

Once the violence had calmed down, he set about trying to retrieve his castle. He drove over to the house and not surprisingly, the castle was no longer in the front garden. He tried to contact the customer - without success. He peered through the living room window, and the kitchen window to see if it was in the house. It was not. He checked the backyard, and no castle could be seen.

By this stage, he was starting to panic, dreading the worst. The following day, he managed to contact the customer, who told him that as soon as the violence flared up, they stopped the party and moved the bouncy castle to the downstairs toilet.

There was a lot of relief all round.

16. One member was lifting an inflatable into his van when he slipped and fell. Unknown to him, he fractured his foot. Despite this injury, he still managed to deliver four bouncy castles and collect three of them, before the pain got so bad that he had to admit himself to hospital.

17. One member told me that he delivered a large slide into a field where there were some horses quietly grazing at the back. He did not think anything of it until he came to collect the slide later in the afternoon. The horses had become amorous and were running around haphazardly, trying to mate with each other. They were running alarmingly close to the slide which by now had been deflated. The member had to wait until nightfall when finally the horses had calmed down enough for him to enter the field and take away the slide. But it meant a long wait!

18. Just thought I would let you know about one of the strangest hires I have ever had.

    On Monday, I received a phone call asking to book one of my bouncy castles preferably a 10ft x10ft unit to a customer in my area. He wanted it for Wednesday till Thursday. I told him I do not do overnight hires and anyhow the weather was to be bad. He told me it is not a problem. It was indoors, "well kind of indoors" - confused I asked him to explain.

It turned out the man had been staying at my local harbour for the last 8 months. He was in the process of turning a large fishing boat into a bed and breakfast establishment. It had now been renovated and had a large cargo area. It is his son's birthday, and he has invited all his chums to a party, he has seen my 10ft x10ft bouncy castle at his son's nursery and knew it would fit.

I thought, "OK why not." On Monday, I arrived at 8.00am, and he had a gangplank down for me, and he lifted the hatch of the cargo hold, it looked great inside. He lowered the castle down with a small crane, and it was set up in no time.

It turned out he wanted to hold the party at sea, but some of the other children's parents were not too keen, so he decided to dock. (It made me think what address I could give to my insurance company if an accident happened or if his boat sank. Would 'lost at sea' be a viable claim for me? He, he, he. Anyway, I forgot about the overnight thing, and at 6.00 pm that evening I returned to pick up the castle. Boy was I in for a shock; it turned out the boat was about a 15-foot drop from the top of the pier. That is why he needed it overnight

I did have a laugh about it though. It turns out they all had a fantastic day, and he has booked me for Christmas and summer next year. And they say worse things happen at sea!

19. I have a funny story from this summer. I delivered a bouncy castle to a cottage in a village in Kent. They are regular customers. A field runs along the side of the garden. I ran the cable from the cottage along the fence. I inflated the castle and left. When I returned the customer told me one of the cows in the field had chewed through the cable whilst the party was in progress. Luckily the cow survived, and the customer had a spare cable he could use. He gave me a replacement cable

because he felt a bit guilty. I have been back to the customer, but now I keep the cable inside the fence.

20. Back in July, we delivered an adult castle to a very large house with a field for a garden! To save time I asked the customer if I could drive the van to the drop point she had agreed to. What I did not realise at the time was the garden was clay based! (Can you see where this is going?)

    After unloading and setting up, I jumped back in the van ready to go, and I got stuck fast in the mud!

    The customer had a Mercedes 4x4 and tried in vain to tow me out but ended up stuck fast herself! Fortunately, she was friendly with the local farmer and got him to tow both of us out with his tractor!

21. Deleted because you would not believe it!

22. I hope this is informative and of interest to BIHA members

    One operator had to deliver two 12ft x 12ft castles to a school in Windsor, Berkshire a few years ago. By coincidence, there were two different schools virtually next to each other, and to make matters worse, they both had their summer fêtes on the same day. Unfortunately, the operator delivered the 2 inflatables to the wrong school. He realised his mistake when he received several frantic calls from the school asking why their castles had not arrived.

    Moral: Never assume that the venue you turn up to is the correct one, always double check first! I have even heard of operators who have turned up a company to set up for a corporate function, only to be told that it was to be held at the other company base 2 miles down the road!

23. I knew from the second I woke up I was going to have one of those days! I had three castles for today, originally four but one I had to

cancel as I found out beforehand that it was a flat and they did not own the ground outside the block. I was worried as she was struggling to get the money as her payments were not in yet and for my castle, etc...

At 7 am I am still sleeping, and my phone rang. It was the sister of the person who wanted the castle at the flats. She wanted to pay for the castle for her sister and said could I still do it. I had to explain again that I could not as I did not have permission to put it on the land as she did not own it. I did offer if she could do it at a friend's house or something. I did not tell her that I did not trust them if they were that strapped for cash as I had recently read the thread on the stolen castle.

9 am - First castle delivery and their garden was way too small for the adult castle, so they offered me an extra £10 (wish I had never bothered now) to drive back and get a smaller castle. I called the next person to check it was OK and they said fine as their party was not till later. I changed the castle and set out to the next.

10:15am Second castle - got there to find they had gone shopping as they thought I was going to be very late! I did say it would only be 10 - 15 minutes Anyway they turned up at 10:40am I called ahead to my next one, and he said not to bother it was my loss I tried to get around him, but he was not having any of it even at a discounted rate he wanted to upset his children.

I only got two castles out, and I had a !*? /* morning. I guess we all have bad days at some point, but this took the !*!* for me.

24. Sunday morning, I and another member of staff went to deliver a bouncy castle to a customer's house.

After the delivery, I phoned the boss (Wibbly) and ORDERED him to phone me back on my mobile. He debated doing this, but curiosity got the better of him. My mobile rang, and I recognised the ringtone as Carmen, which meant it was Wibbly ringing. I answered, and my first words were, "Boss, I ain't Happy!"

Now you may be wondering where this is all leading well, let me enlighten you. Imagine the worst ever booking you have ever done, a few things spring to mind, Bratty children, obnoxious nay violent parents, drunks, teens, dog-poo or horse-poo on the castle. Many possibilities there, but all wrong, Sunday morning I got the weirdest, freakiest, strangest and downright shocking booking you could ever imagine. Oh My Goodness! I hear you all cry, what can be so bad. Let me explain...

I and the other member of staff arrive at the booking; it is a christening. We think no problem, should be easy. How wrong we were! As we arrive, the customer opens the door and says, "Hi, we were waiting for you, the kids are looking forward to the castle." Sounds promising, doesn't it? So I ask, "Where's it going, love?" she says "Just round the back in that garden across the courtyard." I walk over to the fence, taking note of the sign on the gate which says 'Garden of Tranquillity', I should have realised at this point, but no, I thought that's nice, a place for the family to relax. I survey the site and find nothing wrong with it, so I say to the customer, "Where can we plug the extension into?" She says, "How long is your lead? Biting back a rude comment I say, "How long does it need to be as I have 2 x 25-metre extensions." "Well if it is long enough, do you want to put it in the house or the storeroom over there?" I say, "The storeroom is probably better, as you won't have to step over the cable all day." "Fine" she says, "I will just go and open it".

So off to the van I go and start to unload, I hand the extensions to the other member of staff and say, "Go with the lady and plug it in" and off they go. I get everything on site and start setting up. After everything is done I look round for the other member of staff for the electrics, no sign, so round the side of the house to the courtyard I go, no sign, round to the storeroom and I shout to the staff member, they come out of the storeroom still with extension cables in their hands, but their face is white as a sheet. I ask "What have you been up to for all this time?" They respond "B...B...B...B...B...B...B...B..." I say, "What are you on about?" "B...B...Bo...Bo....Bo...Bo," to which I am getting annoyed and said, "Don't bother I will do it." So taking extensions, I go into the storeroom and come straight back out. I shout to the customer who says, "Is there a problem? " I said, "Yes you could say that, come here" taking the customer into the storeroom I say "That is a problem, so is that, and that, but that one is the worst." She says, "Why?"

Now at this point, I must mention that the four that I mentioned above were in fact about 6 foot long, 2 foot high and about 3 foot wide at the largest part. Wood looked a bit like pine, satin-lined lids off, 3 were empty, thank God, but one wasn't. So four chuffing coffins, supposed to be a !*!*!*!* christening in a !*!*!*! funeral parlour. Why did I ever get involved in this business!

So, as you can tell, I was not happy. So, after completing the delivery, I phoned Wibbly, and he does not believe me. He thinks I am on a wind-up, so I said, "You can come and pick up boss." He said, "Fine, not a problem" he thinks he's going to call my bluff.

So around comes the pick-up time, and he says come on then. So we get in the van, he's smirking 'cos he thinks it's a wind-up. We get to booking and customer says, "Hello again." I say, "Hi" and I say to Wibbly, "The electrics are in there" pointing to the storeroom, he says fine and wanders over, walks in and stops, I walk over to see his reaction, only to find the coffins are no longer there. He is grinning like a Cheshire cat and says, " Did you really think I would fall for that?" at which point from behind a curtain comes the undertaker pushing a trolley which has an open casket that is occupied by a recently departed old lady. Wibbly just stares at it as it is wheeled past. When it disappears around the corner, he says, "Let's just pack up and never mention this to anybody ever, OK?" I say, "Sure boss, whatever you say." He then leaves me and walks to the van, climbs into the back, sits down and does not move again until we arrive back at the warehouse. At which point, he enters his office, closes the door and when we go to see if he is alright about 10 minutes later we notice the drinks cabinet is now empty, the 3 empty bottles on the floor explain why Wibbly is a little bit drunk.

So as you can see, I think this now qualifies as the single worst booking ever.

25. Be careful when accepting bookings which are a year or more in advance. The following story shows why:

By the way, this year I had 2 occasions when I arrived with a bouncy castle only to be told on one occasion they had cancelled by leaving a message on an answering machine (although obviously not my answer machine), and the other had forgotten who she had booked with, so as she could not confirm the details, she just re-booked with someone else! I could not charge the first customer anything as it was his word against mine. The second customer admitted it was her fault and we agreed on an amount to cover my costs. The most annoying thing was the fact that it was at the height of the season and I could have hired these castles out several times over!

What did these bookings have in common? - They were both booked in advance, the previous year in fact. Although during busy periods it is not possible to confirm all private bookings, I now make sure that I confirm any which are made a long time in advance.

26. In a BIHA newsletter of about 18 months ago, it was reported that a bouncy castle was set up in a community hall which has wooden decking floor apparently, and the story comes on good authority the person setting up the equipment (not a BIHA member!) attempted to stake down the castle to a wooden floor. By doing so, he caused hundreds of pounds of damage and a great deal of embarrassment to the customer having to explain the situation to an angry caretaker. If you thought that this incidence was a one-off, then you would be wrong, as it has happened again - but this time the customer did it deliberately. A member telephoned me with this most strange story. He set up some inflatables and a marquee in the customers' back

garden, and there was a moderate breeze blowing at the time. The customer was so concerned to make sure that the marquee would not blow down that he asked the member if it would be OK if he was to hit a stake into the wooden decking adjacent to the garden. Somewhat wisely the member refused, and immediately the customer picked up the mallet and started banging the stake in him which penetrated the wooden decking. The member was not impressed with this course of action but though he would relate the story anyway.

27. Another member has reported to me that he set up a bouncy castle in a community centre just before Christmas. All went well and as he was demonstrating the safety points to the customer and pointing out the safety mats, sandbags, do's and don'ts, disclaimers, etc., a 'cowboy operator' came into the hall and set up a bouncy castle without any safety mats or sandbags. Also, to the member's surprise, he did not go over any safety procedures or terms and conditions of hire and disclaimer. The member quizzed him about his public liability insurance, and the reply was, "Ain't got none mate."The member then asked him if he had heard of the British Inflatable Hirers' Association or BIHA for short. He replied that he had not. He then went on to say that although he was a "cowboy operator" he was £5 cheaper than anyone else so what was the problem! Was this man living in the dark ages? The member walked away shaking his head in disbelief at what he had seen and heard.

28. One member reported that he recently sold a second-hand bouncy castle and while he was showing the buyer around the unit he pointed out some small tears on the underside of the castle. The customer was so impressed with his honesty that he gave him £100 extra over and above the asking price of the castle.

29. Another member mentioned a story which I found shocking. He set up some equipment in a private back garden, and the agreed price was £650 for the evening's entertainment. However, later in the morning, all the equipment was set up, and the member went looking for the client to arrange payment of the balance. The client came over, and

although was initially impressed with the equipment he then proceeded to point to and identify every mark, scratch, stain, scuff, dirt and took off an amount of money of between £1 and £5 for every mark on the equipment. After about 10 minutes the customer had identified about 50 marks and deducted £200 from the agreed price. The member was furious and vowed not to deal with this customer ever again.

30. I inflated a box castle for inspection prior to a booking only to find the inside covered in black sticky goo . After a phone call to the previous customer, I found out it was silly string. It took my husband five hours to clean and cost me a booking. It also cost me £20 in tar remover. Has anybody else had the something happen? If so what did they clean it with?

31. The story is as follows and occurred in 2001.

    I ordered 3 brand new castles from a company last year. The castles were 2 months late, no-one answered my calls, and I was getting really worried about having paid up front. Finally, they agreed to deliver to my premises. However, I had a call on the afternoon of the delivery day to say that the driver (an employee of the company) had got to within 15 miles of me, but had had enough driving for the day and was not prepared to bring the castles any further.

    The 3 castles were then dumped (unattended) next to a roadside café, and I had a phone call to say that I had to collect them from there. I had to drop everything and go and collect them. When I arrived, I found to my amazement that my 3 castles were not even left with the staff, but were literally just dumped on the forecourt outside the café. I did retrieve them, and they were OK, but I thought I would mention it. I have dealt with some odd companies but thought this was quite something.

32. About 7 years ago, I delivered a 12ft x 12ft bouncy castle to a house about 20 miles from my home. It was a glorious summer's day, and

the well-dressed customer appeared to be delighted with the inflatable. As usual, on delivery, I asked the customer for payment. She replied that her husband had taken the chequebook with him on a shopping trip, and if I was prepared to wait half an hour, I could have my cheque. However, I was really busy that morning and decided reluctantly to collect my cheque for £85 when I came to collect the castle. In the evening, I drove back to this customer's house and immediately knocked on the front door asking for payment. To my surprise, the customer told me quite bluntly that she would not be paying me any money. I asked her why, and she said that they had had a power cut all day and as a result, the inflatable could not be used and that the party had been a disaster, with all the children being very upset as they were unable to have a bounce. I was really shocked, and I said to the customer, "Why didn't you phone me, and I would have delivered a petrol blower to you." The customer replied that she did not know about petrol blowers, and also did not want to bother me with a phone call.

I then told the customer, that under the circumstances, as it was not her fault that I would not be requesting payment from her.

I walked around to the back of the garden and started to roll up the castle. While I was doing this, the customer's young son (about 5 years old) wandered out into the garden and stood there watching me. After a few moments, I apologised to him for the fact that the power-cut had prevented him and his friends from bouncing on the castle. However, his reply was not what I expected... He looked at me puzzled and said, "What do you mean? We have all been bouncing on the castle all day long - it's been really great fun." I suddenly realised that the customer had lied to me and was trying to con me out of £85. I finished putting the castle back in my van, trying not to get angry, and trying to think of what I was going to say to the customer. I then knocked at her front door a second time and very calmly told her that there had been a mistake and that her young son had just told me that he and his friends had bounced on the castle all day, and please could I have my cheque for £85 as agreed. The customer then told me that her young son must be lying, as she had not had any electricity all day. I then told her that her son seemed happy, and it was extremely unlikely for a 5 year-old child to tell me he had been bouncing all day on the castle, if it was not actually true, so please could I have my cheque. The customer went very quiet for a few seconds and then shouted at me very loudly, "HOW DARE YOU CALL ME A LIAR" and slammed the door on me. I rang the doorbell, but she would not answer the door. By this time I was really annoyed and realised that I had probably been the victim of a con-trick. I drove away empty handed and very shocked and certainly had no idea that I would be sharing this story with hundreds of other hirers many years later.

The moral of this horror story is always try to collect payment on delivery, and never assume that the customer is always telling the truth. If necessary get a second opinion from somebody else. Fortunately, this type of incident is rare, but it can and does happen once every few years. Most customers are a pleasure to do business with.

33. Once we were asked to deliver a bouncy castle to a house on the same day that the booking was made, but when we arrived, we just had a funny feeling about the place. The person came out and said they wanted to pay by cheque (we usually only take cash on the day and had informed them on the phone prior to the booking), for some reason, although there were no visible signs I decided not to leave the inflatable with them. About a week later, I spoke to a colleague and guess what, the same thing had happened to him, but he had left the castle and taken a cheque - when he went back to collect the castle in the evening not only was it gone so had the people. The house was actually empty, and they had installed themselves for a couple of weeks and got away with hundreds of pounds of various items using a mobile phone to order same-day goods. We now have a policy of always taking a land-line number with all bookings - a tip for other hirers maybe?

Start and Run a Profitable Bouncy Castle Hire Business

34. This story involves a customer who set up a bouncy castle on day 2 of her hire, but as it was such a fine day she did not bother to stake the castle to the ground and of course (Murphy's Law), there was a thunderstorm in the afternoon with 70 mile-an-hour winds. The castle and the blower both took off with the blower then crashed to the ground with the cone ripped off the castle and it landed in the next field. The customer then tried to drag it back, all along her gravel driveway, to where it had been set up - but gave up about halfway. Amazingly enough, the only damage done was a slight scratch on one of the walls and quite a considerable amount of mess - mostly mud.

35. We recently had a hire where the customer hired a tall wall bouncy castle with turrets on the four corners. This was an indoor hire, held in a school hall. Whilst setting up the inflatable, all appeared to be fine. However, the tips of the turrets were only just touching the ceiling in the hall. We did not foresee any problems with this at this stage.

    However, upon collection, where the children had been bouncing, the tips of the turrets had worn away the ceiling! (which happened to be a suspended polystyrene one). Oh Dear!

    As it was, the customer had insurance covered by the school, and the damage was paid for, although, he did ask us for a contributory payment to cover the excess fee. We paid this out of goodwill, especially as we knew the customers personally. However, I do feel that they should have either contacted us when it happened or turned the castle off or, ideally, both. It was very apparent as there were considerable 'large flakes of ceiling' falling on them!

    Moral of the story - ALWAYS CHECK YOUR CEILING HEIGHT IF HIRING INDOORS

36. I once delivered a 12ft x 12ft castle to a house that was in the middle of a long row of terraced houses. I was working on my own and going to and fro with the equipment. On about my fourth trip armed with a mallet and stakes I accidentally walked through the wrong door and

found myself in the wrong living room of someone who was not my customer. I realised my mistake immediately -but just as I did the owner of the house came in from the garden, saw me standing in the middle of her living room, screamed at the top of her voice, grabbed a broom and chased me out of her house with it.

I told my customer what had happened and she went round to her neighbour's house to apologise on my behalf. Within minutes, everyone in the entire terraced block had heard what happened -and had a good laugh about it. Although a hiring from hell, I picked up several referrals as a result!

37. This story occurred in the summer of 2001. A hirer delivered a bouncy castle to a customer who had used him regularly in the past. The customer stipulated that he was to get there at 10pm, but no earlier. As it was, he arrived at the customer's house at about 9-45pm just as it was starting to get really dark, and he let himself into the back garden- but the sight that he was greeted with was not quite what he expected. There were 2 men and a woman lying on the bed of the castle, all naked below the waist… it was fairly obvious what had been going on… the woman (who happened to be his customer) got off the castle as soon as he arrived, extremely embarrassed, and doing her best to get her underwear and trousers back on.

38. We had a castle to deliver last year and found the road, and I knocked on the door. "Bouncy Castle," I said to the man who opened the door - with a small lad in tow. "Not 'ere it ain't," he said. The little boy came to the door and saw the van, "Oh wow Dad," he exclaimed. "Please, can I have a castle please, please!" "No you can't," said the man, and slammed the door. Then off we drove leaving one very tearful little boy.

The moral of this story is - always double check when a Road runs adjacent to a Grove and hope that if you choose the wrong number, a little child is not at the wrong one. But it only goes to show that the general public can sometimes be so offhand!

39. My booking from hell, if you like, almost happened this week - I rang the customer to confirm they still wanted the castle due to all the rain we were having, to discover that the booking had actually been made by the ex-husband, in good faith I believe, but the 'children' were actually 15 and 16 years old! As my castle is only 12 ft x 12 ft, I explained that it was not designed for young adults and regrettably we would not be delivering the castle as expected.

    The woman was very understanding (but I expect the 'ex' got it in the neck!) and there was not a problem, fortunately. I guess the lesson learnt is always to ask the age of the children when taking the initial booking. Anybody got any more tips for us rookies?

40. Just a quick note reference a hire I had this weekend. About two months ago I was phoned by a young woman asking for a bouncy castle for young teenagers. Against my better judgement, the booking was taken on the basis of payment up front and a £100 deposit because it was to be left overnight. On the day of the booking the weather was bad, rain all day, we rang the girl, and her dad answered, "Yes, of course, we still want it." So we left it a bit later when the rain had eased and delivered it as requested. The castle was erected on the edge of a part of the garden that he had been trying to grow grass (and failed) because it was so wet. I advised that I would use two ground sheets and some old safety mats, so it was not the end of the world if they got dirty. They asked for the roof to be fitted. I suggested this would not be a good idea as it would be removed soon after I left, but no they wanted it fitting, so fitted it was. On leaving, I gave the father a bag for the roof asking when they take the roof off could he please put it away safely. He agreed and said he would make sure it was looked after and would clean the castle at the end as I was collecting 7:30 am next morning to take it to the next job 9am.

    On arrival next day the castle was uncovered, roof attached by one rope at the back and the general condition of the castle was black. Mud walked all over in shoe prints, not just feet marks. The roof looked like it had been washed in mud. I was gutted! In 4 years I had never seen anything like it. So I decided that I would not return their deposit (something I have never had to do before).

No one was up, so I packed up and left. Then 3 hours later I got a call from the girl, "How do I get my deposit back?" I explained that I would not return her deposit because of the condition of the equipment. She apologised and hung up, but 1/2 hour later dad phoned telling me I had no right to keep their money. I explained everything and that the terms and conditions stated that damage other than fair wear and tear would be charged for. He expressed his opinion that the mess that the castle was in did not constitute damage and I should return his money. After this call my whole day Saturday was taken up by him ringing me threatening trading standards, small claims court, B.I.H.A., and anything else he could dig up.

Then the next thing was the brother-in-law, same sort of thing. On Sunday the dad phoned me again and said this had all got out of hand and could we sort it out? I said as a goodwill gesture to keep the peace I would return £30 as I lost a job for £85 that I was unable to do because of the state of the castle (also the first time in 4 years I have had to let someone down) and the time it took me to clean it I was still out of pocket but if it put an end to his ringing me I was willing to do it. He refused the offer and hung up.

I will be interested if you or anyone else thinks I was right or not. As this is the first time I have done this, I would welcome others' opinions - right or wrong?

41. Another house we arrived at, we inspected the garden for suitability to find 3ft of grass and a bonfire in the middle, and we were expected to wait until they had cleared the garden before being able to put the castle out, we tried to explain fire and plastic do not mix, but in the end we made the excuse the garden was not big enough to house a bouncy castle.

42. I went to pick up my slide/bouncer from a client that has used me before - in fact; I organise discos at her school. When I arrived on this bright sunny day, I was rather surprised to see that the bouncer and the mats were wet. On asking, I was told that the children at the party had been using next door's pool, and must have got the bouncer wet that way. I started looking at the bouncer, and there seemed to be too much water for it just to have been wet children. This rather annoyed me, wet bouncer on a sunny day. There were some clues - water pistols (big ones!) lying around, and water on the very top of the bouncer, a good 15 feet in the air. I am fairly certain that the children had deliberately soaked the bouncer, perhaps to make the slide more slippery.

This may not seem too bad - after all, a wet bouncer is part of the business. The thing to note is that I had got so involved in drying the bouncer and talking to the hirer (it was fairly obvious by this stage that no one had been supervising the bouncer, despite there being a pond in front of it) that I almost did not notice the damage to the bouncer. Where the wall was sewn to the rear arch - it was not! It looks like a kid has created themselves a shortcut to the slide.

End result - I have informed the hirer that she will have to pay for the repair and any loss of earnings, and I have got her to sign to agree. I will be desperately trying to get the bouncer fixed this week. I so nearly missed the damage.

43. This hiring from hell occurred during the Golden Jubilee weekend. A man was bouncing on a child's castle while he was drunk. His knee came up and hit him hard in the face. A few minutes later his face swelled up like a balloon. He went to the hospital, and the doctors found that his cheekbone was broken.

44. In the summer of 1996, I delivered a 12ft x 12ft bouncy castle to a very beautiful, but very old hotel about 12 miles from where I live. It was for a wedding reception, and they wanted it to go inside the hotel, as the weather was a bit unsettled. I inflated the castle, tied the

sandbags to each corner and prepared to drive home. However, I noticed that the top of the castle was only about an inch from the ceiling. I did not think that this would cause any problems. However, I took a closer look at the ceiling and noticed that there were some very powerful light bulbs actually sunken into the ceiling. I realised that if these lights were switched on, there was a possibility that the heat from them could damage the castle. I explained to the customer, that under no circumstances should the lights above the castle be switched on. I also mentioned it to one of the hotel's managers and asked them to put a notice by the light switch.

Later on that day, I arrived back at the hotel to collect the castle. I opened the door, and to my horror, I saw that the light bulbs had been switched on, and smoke was pouring from the top of my castle. I switched the castle off and inspected the damage. At the top of one of the arches, there was a hole about the size of a dinner plate. There were black burn marks on the top of the other arches. Fortunately, I managed to get the castle repaired a week or so later.

45. Two weeks ago I delivered a 12ft x 12ft castle to a house. It was apparent that the site had recently been cleared of brick and rubble. However, not all rubble had been cleared, so I spent 5 minutes picking up all the debris. It was not totally flat, and the area was only just sufficient to site the castle. I put down the groundsheet and had to place the blower on an elevated part of the site in order for the castle to fit. As the castle inflated, it was obvious that a small heavily pruned eucalyptus tree was going to obstruct the castle. The hirer said he would cut down the offending branch; he tried to cut down the branch with an electric wood saw with a small blade. After 5 minutes and very little impression on the branch, the blade broke. He then used a hand saw but again with little impression. I was becoming a little worried since I still had to make 2 more drops and the agreed times were fast approaching. In desperation, the hirer got a pick out of the back of his van and started to dig at the roots. I was helping him by leaning on the stump while he hacked away at the roots. Eventually, 10 minutes later, the tree was uprooted, and I quickly erected and

inflated the castle. The hirer was most apologetic about the incident. When I got back into my car to drive to the next customer, my hands were sticking to the steering wheel and the gear stick, it was then I had noticed that my hands were covered in tree sap!

46. We hirers must have many of these horror stories regarding castle hire. These people hire the inflatable full of promises to look after them read and sign the rules sheet, and within two minutes of our being down the road, they have broken all the rules. One that I remember well is the day we delivered the castle to a young family eager to get bouncing. We situated the castle on the lawn, pegged it down, crash mats were put in place, documents were signed, and we left them to it. One hour later they phoned to say their child had been injured - were we covered by public liability insurance? Obviously yes we were. We were told to fetch the castle back, and they wanted a full refund as the castle had been too highly inflated, and the child had bounced off breaking his leg…"never heard that one before" and they were on the way to the hospital - would we call later in the day to discuss this matter. As it looked like rain, we decided to call and pick the castle up and noticed it had been moved to the pato, a very informative neighbour looked over the fence and said, "Oh are you taking it away, I was told my kids could play on it for the day." I asked the woman why the castle had been moved to the patio and she very kindly told me the children had been jumping out of the *bedroom* window onto it. Guess who did not get a claim form!

47. I have not been in this game a long time, but I have already got a few howlers from taking out the inflatables. You could not include some of this stuff in the best soap opera scripts, but these are TRUE!

    We arrive at an end - terraced house with a 12ft square inflatable which had the previous day, been out in the rain! The man's got a BMW, a trailer, and a 20ft caravan in his drive. Cannot move the caravan, it has got a flat tyre, and there is only an 18 inch gap between the caravan and the house. "No problem," he says "We'll take it through the house!"

We go in through the front door - sack barrow, and wet castle.

It is like a slalom course, through the hallway, into the kitchen, around the refrigerator freezer, and out into the back! Once we set up, we go back through the lounge, and there is a trail of muddy water across the man's carpet. "It's OK", he says, "The missus will clean it up when she gets back from her sister's!"

Exit very quickly, before she gets back!

48. Arrived at another terraced house the other day, the owner says, "The gardens underwater, can you put it up in the house?" The Kid Kube's not that big, so I say, "OK. I'll give it a go."

In her front room, she has moved the three piece suite, and the dining table, so we blow it up. It jams against the fireplace and the opposite wall, and one of my staff is stuck behind it, and cannot get out! "Not to worry," she says "Climb out of the front window!"

49. I had an inquiry a few months ago about an indoor hire to a local village hall. "OK, no problem there," I thought, but as the story unfolded, I could hardly believe my ears. The caller said that her friend had hired a bouncy castle from another hirer and afterwards was handed a large bill for damage to the village hall as the other hire company had amazingly actually staked the castle to the wooden floor of the hall! It must have taken quite some force to ram the steel stakes into the wooden flooring, and I cannot believe that someone would even try it. I can only assume that the hirer was not a BIHA member.

50. We delivered a bouncy castle/ball pond to a party, and they had a large dog who chewed virtually all the balls in the ball pond. Almost every ball had teeth marks on it, and they all had to be thrown away. The crazy thing is that it must have taken the dog hours to chew all those balls. Therefore customer must have known what was going on. The only good thing was that it was a huge relief that the dog did not chew the corners of the actual inflatable.

51. Sometimes it is the hire company which causes a 'Hiring from Hell' - not the actual customer. A shocking story has just come in from a member of the public. She told me that last year she hired a large adult inflatable from a hire company. The bed seams were very worn. As a result, every time an adult bounced on it -their feet would touch the ground. She complained and was told that it was quite normal (By the way, this hire company is NOT a member of the BIHA). Apparently, the adults did not have much fun, and there were lots of sore feet at the end. Definitely a 'hiring from hell'.

52. I picked up my bouncy castle from a very successful five-aside children's football event. It was a fine day, and apparently, over 3000 people attended it. I arrived at 6.00pm - the official finishing time of the event. I could see that there were still masses of people about enjoying the activities. I spoke to the organiser who is one of my best customers. "Shall I come back later when the crowds have gone away?" Living local to the event, it certainly would not have bothered me. He said, "We must start clearing away to indicate the event must close and we all have homes to go to." By removing the large bouncy castle, it would be obvious the event was closing.

Pleasing my best customer, I deflated and packed up the castle. Because the car park was still practically full, I had parked my car and trailer not in the usual convenient place to pick up the castle but the other side of the car park. This did not really worry me because I had got a good sack barrow to take the castle to the other side of the busy car park.

Whilst transporting the heavy bouncy castle on the sack barrow across the car park going between various parked cars, the castle accidentally slipped off the trolley. It fell against a parked car, breaking off the car's wing mirror and scratching the car's doors with the buckle of the strap holding the castle together in its rolled-up state. I had a large audience of children and adults watching me so there was no way I could get away with it. The children are the first people to shout out, "Look what the bouncy castle man's done." I was very embarrassed, and I obviously had to own up. It cost me £150 to get the damaged car fixed.

This whole incident started me thinking just how easily accidents can happen and just how vulnerable hirers are. We all think it will never happen to us. I was fortunate that I could afford to pay up. If you stop to think about it, the cost could have been much more. I am not insured for such accidents, and I am sure not many other hirers are.

The castle may also have slipped off the trolley as I was passing many young children sitting on the grass at the event. Where would a hirer stand if a child got injured from equipment being carried to and from an event? Many a time I have picked up a castle from a party and the children are really enthusiastic to help. What if a child accidentally falls against the blower as you are carrying it to your vehicle? I have my doubts if public liability insurance would pay out for anyone getting injured from moving equipment. I have probably opened a whole can of worms for hirers to think about as they move their inflatables and equipment. The main advice I can give any hirer is - BE CAREFUL! It is easy, after the event to look back and think, "I should have done so and so differently or not at all."

53. A story came in recently which I found disturbing. A customer of a BIHA member hired a brand new adult-sized bouncy castle for a typical back-garden party. The party was an all-nighter, and at 3am the party was still in full swing, with loud music blaring out. However, one of the neighbours became irate with the noise and apparently crept into the garden, armed with a Stanley knife and ripped a huge tear along the inflatable, causing £700 worth of damage. Apparently, the attack on the unit was so ferocious that it caused several layers of the material to be damaged. The police were called, but no-one owned up to this act of vandalism.

54. We had to deliver our biggest castle, a 15ft x 16ft adult unit, to a long narrow garden. At the front end of the garden on the left was a large fish pond and on the right was a small marquee, leaving a narrow gap

to get to the rest of the garden. We picked it up quite late at night, and there was little light. As we went between the pond and marquee, yep, you guessed it, the wheel on the sack barrow slipped over the side on the pond, and before we could grab it, the castle rolled over into the pond, which turned out to be 6 ft deep. Well, 'wet castle' does not really cover it. Although we could just reach the straps under the water, there was no way we could lift it, even an inch. Luckily a friend of mine has a lorry with a HIAB crane, and there was a lane running down the side of the garden. The next day we went round and hoisted it out of the pond and over the fence. Luckily the castle had very stout webbing straps, as we reckon it weighed over one and a half tons.

55. One member has told me that he supplied a petrol blower to a bouncy castle booking, and the rain-cover came down and accidentally blocked the vent on the side of the blower. To keep the inflatable correctly inflated the customer moved the throttle to full power (and did not move the rain-cover) out of the way. For over an hour the blower screamed at maximum revs until all the fuel ran out.

56. A member has e-mailed me a rather amusing story. He was setting up an inflatable in a customer's back garden. Suddenly, he wanted to have a wee. So, he asked the customer if he could use the toilet. The customer (a man) said that he could go against a tree in the garden, as he had just had a brand new downstairs bathroom fitted. Fortunately, he declined the offer of a tree as the customer's wife was in the house -and it would not have looked very professional if his wife had looked out of the window or come out to hang up the washing.

57. We were delivering a foam-sided ball pond to a house that was near the top of a steep hill. There was no drive, so we had to park the van on the road. Got the ball pond into the house and set it up, then back to the van for the balls. They are kept in a couple of large nets hanging from hooks in the roof. As I pulled the first one out, the tie caught on a snag and pulled open. Before I could react, 1000 balls went cascading down the hill. It took about an hour to collect up all the balls that had not been run over!

58. Here is a true story told to me by one of my London customer's Martin [a proper cocky cockney].

He arrived at this very large house to deliver a bouncer for a birthday party, on knocking at the door he was greeted by a well-spoken woman in her mid-thirties who informed him that she had prepared an adequate space for him to erect the inflatable at the rear of the house and he was to use the side entrance. Martin rushed around to the back of the house with his bouncer on the sack truck and spotted a large tarpaulin laid out in one corner of the garden. So he ran to the edge of it and pushed the bouncer on to it, turns around and returns to his van to fetch the blower, stakes and extension lead. When he returned to the garden, his bouncer had disappeared. On closer inspection he found his bouncer sitting at the bottom of the biggest garden pond you have ever seen (which the tarpaulin was covering).

He then had to explain why he had thrown his bouncer into her pond, apologised, and waded into 3ft of smelly pond water to retrieve it. Luckily the owner saw the funny side of it and made him a cup of tea and gave him a towel to dry off.

Moral: Always check what is going to go underneath the castle.

59. I delivered a bouncy castle for a customer (15 miles away), and it was to go in their large double garage. Before I set off, I asked the customer the height, and she said 18 feet. I thought no problem - but there were rafters and beams about 8 feet above the ground - as a result, the castle did not fit, and I had to drive 15 miles home and get a smaller unit.

Moral: If you are driving a long distance to a venue which you are unfamiliar with always try and take a smaller unit in case the first unit does not fit.

60. I had many calls last season requesting an adult bouncy castle, the most interesting from a woman who was holding a divorcee party.

I asked, "Why do you require a bouncy castle?" To which she replied, "I've invited five of my divorced girlfriends and four divorced males and thought we would have a few beers and when it gets dark get on the castle and see what happens." Over the phone my mind boggled, I explained I only had a 12ft x 12ft, though she needed something bigger. Over the season I recorded 25 requests for castles for people over the age of 18.

This is useful as they realise they cannot go on the normal children castles as they will damage them.

61. The day before I went to Florida, I carried out a site inspection for a customer who wanted two bouncy castles and two marquees. Not surprisingly, I was in a very happy mood. I quoted her £500, but I then said to her, I'm in such a good mood, as I'm going to Florida in the morning, I'll give you £100 DISCOUNT." She smiled at me and agreed to this price immediately.

Moral: The more cheerful you are on the phone or in person - then the more likely that your enthusiasm will be infectious and your customer is more likely to book, then perhaps make further bookings later.

62. A hirer was staking an inflatable down whilst the children were still playing on it. Some children threw themselves at the side wall quite violently, and the hirer was thrown backwards several feet.

Fortunately, he was only winded, but it could have been much worse.

Moral: If you are staking an inflatable down - make sure that the children are not bouncing on the unit.

63. I had a unit out at the weekend, and the customer was perfectly happy with everything as we left. Nearing pick-up time, he rang the office and said that they wanted to keep the unit longer as - "...the kids haven't been able to go on it all day as the plug was sparking." My driver turns up, inspects everything and all seems well, so he leaves it

another half-an-hour and now the customer is saying he is not happy and wants a FULL refund. The driver then refers him to the office.

The story he uses on me is a cracker. He was not issued with a top copy invoice with our emergency numbers on. (He did get one!). He has been trying the office number all day to get someone to go and look at the unit (NO messages on answerphone, 1571 or my mobile, which is on all the time!) He then said the driver signed the top copy (which earlier, he said he had never received) to say he could have a full refund. The driver knew nothing about that! I have asked to see the top copy, and I will bet there has been some falsification going on here somewhere!

Needless to say, I am hanging on to the money!

64. Don't you just love this job! One person phoned a member recently, and the conversation was as follows: "I have booked a bouncy castle with a company in Berkshire, but I cannot remember which company it was." "How much were you quoted?" "I can't remember." "What size did you order?" "I can't remember." "What was the theme of the inflatable?" "I can't remember, but it may have had a rocket on the top." At this point, I said that I could not help, and said, "Goodbye." This type of call happens several times every year. Imagine the same thing happening to a travel agent. "Excuse me; I wonder if you can help, I have booked a holiday with some travel agents in my local town, but I can't remember which one." "Where is the destination, sir?" "I can't remember." "How much you have paid sir?" "I can't remember", and on and on and on. One BIHA member hired out a castle for a group of children, and they showed their 'appreciation' by signing their names on the unit with a biro pen.

65. We went to a delivery a few weeks back with our slide. No problem at all until we went to pick it up on the night. Going through the gate, there was a tearing noise. Sure enough, there was a 9-inch hole in the bottom of the slide. Upon further investigation we found screws sticking out of the gate. We had not seen them when we delivered, so

we asked the customer about it. "Oh yes," he said, "I've put new hinges on the gate today, and I've used bigger screws, and they stick out a bit." What can you do?

66. Had this happen just this morning!

Paving slabs, wheelie bin, children' toys, and a pile of soil right where the customer wants the castle. "I tell you what; I'll come back later when you've moved the mound." The customer then gets on his high horse! What do they expect, you are going to grab a spade and help them move it?

When we confirm a booking, we always state that they must 'prepare' access routes for the delivery team. Just this weekend I had to squeeze an inflatable past two dustbins and promptly snagged it on a ladder covered in paint.

67. Amazing isn't it?

I had a customer once hand me a spade when I pointed out his dog had messed all over the lawn. (To the best of my knowledge the spade is still where I threw it down).

68. I turned up to a booking and had to negotiate a rusty old car with flat tyres leaving about a 2 ft gap between it and the wall; the gate had a pile of paving slabs, which had to be moved so it could open fully. The hiring area was not safe nor big enough for the castle, despite explaining the dimensions of the castle and the need for extra space around and especially in front for safety. So we (mostly I) had to move:
    scaffolding
    bikes and toys
    wet manky tarpaulin
    rabbits
    rabbit hutches (6 ft hutches)
    rabbit excrement

rusty tubular frame double swing
piles of bricks
a load of other stuff, I now cannot remember and I had to take down the washing line.

The castle was now opened out partly onto concrete, so I got my groundsheet and safety mats. When finished the castle was lovely and safe with no dangerous objects around or in front. Despite this the people hiring were furious that they had to do all this, each thing that needed to be moved got them angrier.

Here is the best bit:

This all took well over an hour. At 12noon I went through the Hire agreement and asked for payment. They asked for a discount on a £40 hire because I had said the castle takes 20minutes to set up and they would now have it for less time!

I look back on that day and think, "What the hell was I doing - never again." I now explain to all my customers on booking and on the follow-up call the need for clear areas and clear access. No matter how much I explain I still end up moving kid's toys and wheelie bins, but I do it with a smile as I remember the above booking.

69. One BIHA member told me how one of her customers dismantled the equipment at the end of the party and brought it all out onto the front garden where it remained for several hours before they came to collect it. It was only a miracle which prevented a passing motorist from stopping and stealing the equipment. Our customers must be better educated to look after our equipment!

70. I had a funny experience today. I received a call from a customer wanting an inflatable for next weekend. I told him what we had, and he asked if we could do a discount on two items. I agreed and quoted him the price. He said he would call back in half an hour. He did and asked for an extra £5 off. Reluctantly I agreed, and as I started to take

his address I thought, "He's having me on," as he gave me a house name which was unusual and then told me he lived on Cuckoo Cage Lane!

At this point, I thought, "Yes and I'm Noddy." So I put the phone down thinking I was being wound up. Luckily I never gave him any abuse as when I got to my mother's house and told her she laughed and said, "That really is a place!"

So I phoned the man back, and he said, "Oh I know your battery went flat whilst on the phone." I agreed of course as the customer is always right.

Fortunately, I got the booking and am now being called a numpty. I am glad I never gave him any stick when he initially gave me his address!

BIHA Tips of the Week

These tips have been sent out to the members of the BIHA for many years. Here is the pick of the crop. They are edited slightly for the purposes of this book.

BIHA Tip 1
There has been some talk on the discussion forum recently about the spending habits of customers who hire bouncy castles from us. Some customers have an almost limitless budget when it comes to making a success of their child's special day. Also, some parents are keen to show off and impress their friends. According to a study carried out by Cussons (and endorsed by the Daily Mail) 10% of parents now spend more than £250 on food, gifts and entertainment for an under-12's party.

This means that if you are charging the standard rate of say £50 to £85 for a 12ft x 15ft bouncy castle, then for at least 10% of your customers you are potentially leaving a great deal of money on the table!

I recently came across this short article in the National Press. It does make interesting reading - and shows the folly of putting out bouncy castles for ridiculously low hire fees such as £30 to £40 per day. Some of my own customers used to tell me that by hiring a bouncy castle they did not need to spend money on other things - apart from food, drink and party bags. The inflatable was THE entertainment.

If the article below is anything to go by, then the customer's who hire bouncy castles would be willing to pay more if prices were increased across the board.

> The average cost of a children's Party.
> Back in the old days a game of pass the parcel, musical chairs followed by Jelly and Ice Cream was all that was expected from a children's birthday party.

However, nowadays, parents are so keen to impress their friends that the average cost of a birthday party has soared to £152.

10% of parents now spend more than £250 on food, gifts and entertainment for an under-12's party.

One in five parents has even admitted to spending more than £40 just on party bags!

Parents are more likely to spend the most money on their child's fifth birthday, according to a study by Cussons.

It found that 30% of parents now feel that their child's special day is 'very competitive' - with only one in seven not believing that there was any pressure to compete with other birthday parties.

A small number of parents (7%) will even start planning the big day as much as 6 months ahead.

Source: Daily Mail (2014)

BIHA Tip 2
During the course of a typical week, I get to talk to several BIHA members, and one of the topics sometimes raised is how they are getting bookings. In the early years of the BIHA, members used to say the Yellow Pages, then a few years ago, it was mainly from their website.
Nowadays, members tell me that a significant proportion of their bookings come from Facebook and other social media sites, in addition to their own website.

Moreover, posting on Facebook, Google +, Twitter, Instagram, Linked In, etc., can be extremely time-consuming although it has been proven to help you streamline your marketing and help you get more bookings!

So, is there a tool which can automate this task? Happily, there is! It is called HOOTSUITE, and is free for up to 3 social media sites. There is an 8-minute video which explains how to use it at this URL: https://youtu.be/CfP_Av0NAwM

The website is at https://hootsuite.com

BIHA Tip 3
I have often discussed how one can increase the results of marketing using testimonials to build credibility. To review, click on over to my blog to read the first two entries.

If you are just starting out in your business or have a brand new product, you can give your new product or service to people you trust, who in turn can use it in return for a promise to give you a testimonial. Or, if you have testimonials from a previous business or product/service, but not this new venture, you can re-tool your existing testimonials to work for your new venture.

For example, a window washer is adding window installation service; you can quickly and easily make the 'old' testimonials work for the new 'new' business, especially testimonials about service, quality, or a certain person in the business who still works with you. Most of those will remain true in your new venture.

Using testimonials is the biggest method to gain credibility, but there are other ways as well.

First, you can list the accomplishment, awards, articles, book published, etc. In the late 1990's, a business, the American Retail Supply, won the award as the 'Best Small Business to Work for in Washington State' by a Washington Business Journal. We used that advantage for years, and still use it from time to time today.

A new book was also written, 'Out Nordstrom Nordstrom's: 57 Secrets to Make-You-Happy Customer Service', and we use that all the time.

Another great strategy is to use pictures. Pictures are vitally important because they allow you to use captions, which is the third most-read part of any type of advertisement. Use before/after pictures when appropriate, or any kind of picture that can relay a story. Many of my Real Estate clients use pictures of their happy home sellers or buyers standing in front of the 'Sold' sign. Think about how you can use pictures in your marketing!

BIHA Tip 4
During an unusually cold spell, it is advised that you inform your customers and potential customers of all the halls that they can hire in your local area. Children have birthdays every day of the year, and if it is too cold to have a castle or slide in their back garden then many children will still insist on having an inflatable, but the parents will prefer to hire a hall. You can use two methods to help encourage your customers to hire halls rather than cancel the party if they think it is too cold for outdoors.

1) Display on your website (in a very prominent place) all the local halls in your area including their contact phone numbers and contact name. Then, when they ring to enquire about hiring inflatables, you can mention the list of halls on your website, and hopefully, encourage them to book one.
2) Contact all the caretakers of these halls, and introduce yourself and your services and explain that you can pass leads to them, especially when the weather is unusually cold. Perhaps offer to make a small donation to the hall fund. (Some need new roofs, etc., so offering a donation often goes down well).

Some caretakers will recommend you to parents who contact them enquiring about hiring a hall.

BIHA Tip 5
Email Marketing
If you want to increase the profits of your inflatable hire business and gain more customers. Then it is important that you are using email marketing to communicate with your prospective customers and your existing customers. Unfortunately, many inflatable hire businesses are still yet to

fully utilise email marketing, and some of them are still doing it incorrectly.

In this BIHA Tip of the Week, I am going to explain to you how you can use email marketing effectively for your business and gain more customers and build a relationship with them. Every time you make a booking, offer the customer an incentive to give you their email address. For example, a free garden game hire or 10% discount off their next booking in return for their email address.

In addition, you can add an 'opt-in form' to your website encouraging your customers and prospects to sign up to your monthly or quarterly newsletters, or special deals, or last-minute booking discounts, etc.

Once a customer or prospect enters their name and email address (i.e. 'opts in'), they will automatically be added to your mailing list.

Once you start building up a collection of email addresses, you can start putting it to work and start communicating with them on a regular basis, with the idea of getting more bookings and referrals.

This idea can work surprisingly well. E.g. if you have an unexpectedly-quiet weekend, and the sun comes out, you can email your entire list of customers and prospects, (pretty much for free if you use www.MailChimp.com) and offer them a special deal if they hire from you at short notice. The chances are that at least 3 or 4 customers will take you up on your offer, especially if their children need to be kept busy while they do other things, e.g. DIY/decorating, etc.

Also, some parents will organise a last-minute barbeque or another social event where they need their children (and their friend's children) to be kept occupied! If you have just sent them an email, you will be uppermost in their mind should they decide to hire an inflatable - be it now or later in the year.

Try to make your content shareable. If you are sending content to your customers then make sure they have an option to 'share' your content on social media sites such as Facebook. This will help extend the reach of your message.

DON'T SPAM! Whatever you do, please do not spam. Spam is unsolicited email, and if you are found spamming people just to promote your hire business, then you could find yourself in legal trouble. So please avoid this at all costs!

Email marketing can help you gain valuable feedback from your customers. This can help you to see what you are doing correctly and what areas you can improve to help meet the needs of your customers.

Give your customers and prospects the option of being able to 'opt-out' of receiving your emails. E.g. their children may have grown up and left home, and they may no longer need to hire an inflatable from you.

According to the Direct Marketing Association for every £1 spent on email marketing the 'return on investment' (ROI) has been £46, so it is well worth doing! Probably the lowest-cost service to organise an email marketing campaign for a business is MailChimp: **www.mailchimp.com**

For your first set of customers who opt-in, the cost is ZERO, and even when you have to start paying, it will probably be surprisingly inexpensive compared to the increase in profits it can bring you.

Here are some of the other services you can use to automatically collect the email addresses of your customers and prospects.

Constant Contact http://www.constantcontact.com/uk/index.jsp
Aweber - http://www.Aweber.com
Get Response - http://www.getresponse.com

If you have any problems setting up this email service, please refer to the discussion forum on www.BouncyCastleOwner.com, and I will explain in more detail how to set it all up.

BIHA Tip 6

While I was manning the BIHA stand at a Bouncy Castle Trade Show in the UK Midlands, I had a steady stream of BIHA members (and some non-members) approach me to discuss the industry, SEO, etc., and some of them shared a number of interesting tips and ideas that are working for them to bring more profits into their hire businesses.

Here are 20 of the tips mentioned in no particular order. (Please note that some are for beginners only, others are for intermediate-hire companies and the remainder for long-established hire companies. Something for everyone, I hope).

1) Give refrigeration magnets to your customers after each hire and watch them magically promote your business! Once it is attached, they will see it several times each day. And so will their visitors who enter the kitchen. No other advertising can come close to this! The man who reminded me of this tip has said that he still gets bookings from magnets that he gave to his customers 10 years ago!

2) On the subject of magnets, if you are worried about getting your van broken into, use magnetic van stickers to promote your business. Remove the magnets from the van at the finish of your last job, so no one can follow you home to your lock-up, garage or another place of storage.

3) On your website and marketing materials write these words very clearly "PLEASE BOOK YOUR INFLATABLE EARLY TO AVOID DISAPPOINTMENT." By creating scarcity, you are likely to get more business because people will not want to miss out.

4) At the start of the new hire season, do not just email all your existing customers (from last year and previous years) but send them a mail-shot in the post. One member did this last year and wrote a letter to 600 customers, and the resulting bookings kept his business booming for the following season. (The mail-shot to 600 customers cost him around £400 or so, but the result was well worth the expense).

5) If you have not done so already get both your phone number and your website address on the front step of your bouncy castles. (This provides free advertising and furthermore helps deter theft).

6) If you want inexpensive business cards and flyers, etc., consider contacting VistaPrint.

7) If you want to retain the value of your inflatable, ALWAYS use a groundsheet. Many hire companies (even long-established) do not bother, and as a result, the underside becomes scuffed, grubby and sometimes ripped. When the castle is rolled up, these defects will show and reduce its resale value.

8) One member told me that the best tip that the BIHA can ever give is to recommend that members get a website built by www.BouncyCastleNetwork.com and its diary and booking system or just a website on its own.

9) Visit Bouncy Castle Trade Shows (e.g. INPAS and the Leisure Supplies Show). See the inflatables for yourself and meet the manufacturers all under one roof.

10) Use the forum at www.BouncyCastleOwner.com It is a useful resource, and it is unfortunate that more hire companies do not take advantage of it.

11) We all know about didi cars for toddlers, but what about the older children? The perfect add-on hire product for them is: 'RAZOR RIP RIDERS 360's'. Incredible fun for the slightly-older children and a profitable add-on hire product.

12) Join the BIHA! - at www.biha.org.uk You will get many hundreds of tips to help you run a more profitable and successful hire business, and be part of a lively community of inflatable-hirers. And we also help members get their websites higher up in Google (First come first served)

13) At the Pineapple Show recently someone came up with a very interesting 'upsell' idea. As you may know, Pineapple Leisure sells crash mats with themed artwork printed on them. The idea is to RENT out these crash mats as an upsell HIRE PRODUCT, e.g. for £3 to £5

or more per party. If the customer wants a crash mat with no artwork on it - then it is free, but if they want a themed crash mat, it costs £3 to £5 per day. Such a simple idea because you have to deliver crash mats anyway! So it is no extra work! This idea on its own (as an upsell) could bring in an extra £20 to £50 per week!

14) Sometimes a bouncy castle will be sited at the WRONG ANGLE so that the adults when sitting down, are unable to view the children while they are playing on the inflatable. Then the adults may decide to move the castle at a different angle by unpegging it and turning it a few degrees. Frequently they either forget to stake it down again or do it incorrectly which can scuff and damage the anchor point material against the peg and create a safety hazard. So, do not just ask where the customer wants the inflatable sited. Find out exactly where they will be sitting to watch the children during the party.

15) Make sure you always add a promotional video to your website to greet your visitors. If you forget to do this -you could be missing out on new business. Here is an example promotional video I did for a member at INPAS: http://youtu.be/T4G_AFAmMjk

16) Consider having another 'arm' to your business where you are also providing the whole party package, e.g. mascots, didi-cars, pop-corn, candyfloss, face painting, marquees, etc. There are approximately 200 other ideas on http://bit.ly/1zD2DKR

17) Never provide a bouncy castle or another inflatable for free! (Or think very carefully about it!) There is a small risk that any incident leading to a claim could affect your insurance. It is better to charge £1.00 than nothing. (NOTE: The BIHA has not yet confirmed the validity of this tip). However, the law says that for a contract to be in place there must be 'consideration'. In other words, you provide the kit in return for a fee. If you do not receive a fee, then consideration may not apply, which can change the validity of the contract and possibly your PLI. (N.B. The law of Tort does not require consideration).

18) With the customers' permission, take professional photographs of their children playing on your inflatables and use a high-quality camera, frame the prints, and sell them to the customers, and even the

customers' guests. (Ensure the name and contact details of your hire business are clearly displayed).

19) Consider investing in some MASCOTS as an add-on hire product. Good money earner and can command quite high fees. Consider using students or fit OAP's, etc., to wear these mascots.

20) When you get your happy customers to give you a video review (you can use your smartphone to do this and then upload it to YouTube). Make sure you that you also transcribe what they say and add it to your website under your Customer Reviews section. Some people will then read the text version of the review, even if they do not actually watch the video. Another benefit -it is more content, which Google loves!

BIHA Tip 7
Some inflatable hire companies make the mistake of driving their prices down and down thinking that they are likely to get more bookings and take business away from their competitors.

This can lead to profits being squeezed to the bone such that no funds are then available for repairs and stock rotation, etc. One of the easiest ways to prevent your potential customers from price-shopping is to give them something they cannot get anywhere else!

Examples could be castle/slide combi-units, detachable artwork panels to match the theme of their party, an all-pink castle for girls, offering face-painting, soft play or didicars, etc., alongside inflatable hire, Santa's grottos in the winter.

For more ideas of what you can offer your potential customers that your competitors do not offer - please watch this video of the Leisure Supplies Show held in the West Midlands.

www.youtube.com/watch?v=KURFs9AcTKE

Distinguishing yourself from your competitors (in the eyes of your prospects and customers) can be a highly profitable move!

BIHA Tip 8
The tip this is about five referral systems that you can use for your inflatable hire business to attract more customers.

a) How To Get Referrals from Customers, (Past and Present).
b) Other Inflatable Hire Companies.
c) Non-Competing Businesses In Your Area, (e.g. Face Painters)
d) Local Businesses in your town.
e) Miscellaneous Sources To Refer Their Family, Friends And Co-Workers, etc. To Your Inflatable Hire Business.

Customers who come to your business as referrals from existing or past customers are usually more loyal and committed to your hire company than those who become customers through your usual advertising channels.

Referrals are one of the best ways to build a thriving hire business, and you should do everything possible to attract them. Sadly, an estimated 90% of inflatable hire businesses do not have systems in place to generate referrals for their business.

Why many Inflatable Hire Companies do not receive any referrals:
While there are many benefits to developing systems to generate referrals, you should first make sure your hire business is poised for success. Here are some of the reasons why many hire companies are not positioned for success when it comes to generating referrals.

- They have no real commitment to getting referrals.
- They do not even remember to ask for referrals.
- They are really not doing something unique or different that customers, etc., can recommend to other people.
- Their customer service is poor.
- They are afraid of asking for referrals.

Five main types of Referral Systems:
As mentioned above, there are FIVE main types of referral systems that you will need to have in place in your hire business in order to systematically and consistently generate referrals all the year round:

1. Current (and past) customers: In particular, your existing active customers and fans, e.g. customers who rave about your hire business on Facebook.
2. Other inflatable-hire businesses: Businesses that have sent referrals to you before or to which you have passed referrals.
3. Non-competing local businesses in the entertainment industry, e.g. Face-painters, Party-Bag suppliers, Marquee-Hire companies.
4. Local Businesses: Businesses and organizations with which you can form strategic marketing alliances, e.g. local businesses that you frequent, friends and family who own local businesses, etc.
5. Miscellaneous referral sources, e.g. Schools, Playgroups, Churches, Corporate Bodies, the local Asian community, etc.

Referral System #1: - Customer Referral System
The first step in generating referrals is to start by informing your current customers that you are looking for new customers. Flyers or banners on your website, etc., are helpful as reinforcement tools, but they are *passive* reminders and do not engage or inspire the customer directly.

Many hire companies feel uncomfortable asking for referrals, so simply letting the customer know that you are now 'accepting new customers' is a non-threatening way to plant the referral seed.

The good thing about using that simple statement - "we are now accepting new customers" is that it does not sound patronising or contrived. It is just an honest statement that rings true to both you and the customer. If you combine that with two or three referral cards, you have just created a simple little system that can generate new customers every month.

Referral Systems #2 and #3:
How To Consistently Generate Referrals From Other inflatable Hire Businesses In your local area, and non-competing entertainment businesses (E.g. Face-painters).

When it comes to generating referrals from other inflatable hire businesses, they need to trust you and feel that you are competent and believe you are successful. In other words, you need to have a real relationship which requires time and attention to maintain and grow.

They want to be confident that the referral they pass on to you will be beneficial to their customer's care, and reflect well on themselves. Other hire companies will refer with confidence when there is a strong and reliable relationship in place, especially if the customer is slightly outside their catchment area, or if they are simply too busy or stretched to honour the booking.

Relationship building begins by reaching out to your potential referral sources to learn how and if you can serve their needs. After you have listened, you can begin to tell them about your hire business and your ideal customers.

Regardless of the type of referral providers you are targeting, there are some common threads that dictate their expectations for their referral partners.

- High quality of service and inflatables. You must have a well-established reputation for treating your customers (especially those referred to you) with respect and being ultra - reliable.
- Thank the referring company and tell them that you appreciate the referral.

Case study A: When I was hiring inflatables in the 1990's, I formed a strategic alliance with a company that supplied Party Bags. I passed the owner's details on to my customers, and they reciprocated. This arrangement helped me to grow my business.

Case Study B: During this same period of time, I also formed a strategic alliance with another local inflatable hire company. When the owner was really busy, or his vans were outside his usual catchment area he referred bookings to me, and I returned the favour when *I* had too many bookings. Or there were geographical challenges. I also ran a marquee-hire business where we referred business to each other on occasions.

Referral System #4:
How To Build Your Referral Generating System That Gets Referrals From Local Businesses (aka. Strategic Marketing Alliances).

When two businesses work together to create a joint-marketing campaign that benefits or drives customers to both businesses, it is called a 'strategic marketing alliance'. This *can* be done by mailing letters of recommendations or endorsements to each other's customers and prospects. Regardless of the specific strategy used, the principle is that two different businesses are helping each other to become more successful.

Strategic alliances are very effective ways of obtaining customers on a consistent basis, but this strategy requires you to step outside your comfort zone in order to succeed. That is why probably 99.9% of inflatable hire companies do not even try to use this powerful business building strategy.

Referral System # 5:
Miscellaneous Referral Sources, e.g. Caretakers, schools, Churches, charities, local Asian Community, etc.

Case Study C: I used to be friendly with several local caretakers who looked after community centres in my town. They regularly referred customers to me who had booked a hall with them.

Case Study D: I used to hire my castles to local schools for 'Sponsored bounce' purposes. The school referred my business to parents who were interested in hiring the same castle for their child's birthday party.

Case Study E: I once knew the owner of a hire company who provided excellent hire service to a customer who was a member of the local Indian community in Southall, near Heathrow Airport. Word spread like wildfire that he was reliable and his prices were fair, and within weeks his diary filled up with referrals from this community.

IMPORTANT NOTE: Whenever you receive a referral from any of the above sources, please always try to thank the person who has referred the customer (or customers) to you. This 'thank you' will pay dividends!

BIHA Tip 9 - Another Hiring from Hell

All members can learn from it, and hopefully, save them from a £1,000 repair bill in the process! The operator delivered a bouncy castle to a community centre that he had not been to before.

Unfortunately, the top of the castle was slightly higher than the suspended ceiling, which was made of polystyrene tiles! The customer was happy about this, and the operator thought that the rubbing of the castle against the tiles would not cause any major problems.

However, the continual movement against the ceiling caused extensive damage to the tiles. The castle also moved around which exacerbated the problem. The damage came to over £1,000, and the owner of the hall is suing the operator.

Two lessons are to be learnt from this horror story.
1) Suspended ceiling tiles are quite fragile and castles touching them can cause expensive damage.
2) If you are delivering a castle to a hall with which you are unfamiliar (especially if the customer or caretaker is uncertain of the ceiling height) take an additional castle which has less height, so that you can substitute it if the ceiling is too low.

BIHA Tip 10

Testimonials are great -but how can you actually believe them! Some are no doubt made up, and potential customers know this. Getting pictures of customers and videos of them giving a testimonial can be really tricky at the best of times. My idea is to use Case Studies. In other words, if you write about a booking that you did (either recently or in the distant past), then it does not really matter.

A case study might comprise the following:
1) The name of the street and the customer's first names.
2) The type of inflatable they hired out.
3) Ideally a picture of the inflatable.

4) Perhaps some background as to why they chose you and not your competitors.
5) Perhaps a testimonial or review from the customer.
6) A video and picture of the customer would be advantageous but is not essential.
7) A short description as to how the booking went and what interesting events occurred, e.g. a Face-Painter or clown turning up. The customer is paying for an extra hour because the children were enjoying the bouncy castle so much!

If you do the case-study about a booking you did for a local charity, a well-known local blue-chip business or better still a local celebrity then the power of the case-study is even stronger. Why are case-studies so powerful? And how will they give me more *paying customers?*

There are two ways that case-studies can be a 'game-changer' for your business.

Firstly, customers love 'social proof'. In other words, if they see that you have served other people in the same town with their inflatables, then it makes you look really well-established and that you will turn up on the big day! They are likely to trust you more, and possibly choose you over a competitor who may not have any case studies on their website. In the same way that saying you are a member of the BIHA and the FSB, etc., raises your professional credibility in the eyes of your potential customers, so does publishing case-studies on your website.

Secondly, as mentioned, people lie about testimonials or use their friends and neighbours to write them. However, with case-studies (if done properly) they are 100% authentic and cannot be staged or contrived.

Thirdly, and possibly most importantly, case-studies add all-important content to a website. As you probably know Google loves fresh, original quality-content and will reward sites that have it with higher rankings.

Usually, a higher ranking in Google means that your potential customers can find you more easily, and therefore book you!

You can see this case-study idea in action at **www.WebsiteRentals.biz** (Real-life case-studies at www.WebsiteRentals.biz/case-study-1)

You can also see some demo case-studies for the purpose of this week's BIHA Tip at www.locksmithBracknell.com (This is a site I have just started for a client). The actual demo case-studies can be read online at: : www.locksmithBracknell.com/case-studies-1

As a result, my including case-studies has resulted in a surge of extra website clients for me -not so much bouncy castle hire companies but other individuals such as locksmiths, landscape gardeners and accountants.

So, I would strongly recommend that you include case-studies on your website (and other promotional literature) you should see your bookings increase as a result.

If you are unsure on how to do this -please join in on the thread at **www.bouncycastleowner.com**. Feel free to ask any questions.

The more detailed the case-study, the better and if you can use well-known venues and people and charities, etc., the effect will be that much stronger. Do not forget that in some circumstances you may need to ask permission from the customer to write a case-study of their booking -but nine times out of 10 they will not object and even feel honoured in some cases! They may even give you extra information for the case-study, e.g. a selfie-picture or a video testimonial!

BIHA Tip 11
If your website does not have an opt-in box, you have no way of collecting the names and contact details of the people who visit it and who (for whatever reason) do not hire an inflatable from you. This oversight will almost certainly cost your hire company money in terms of lost bookings and also lost referrals.

This is because you will not have any way of getting in contact with them once they leave your website.

BIHA Tip 12

ALWAYS advertise your inflatable hire business on the BACK of your van and not just the sides.

The reason for this is simple. Any vehicle following your van will have time to read about your hire business and perhaps even view your website on their smart-phone! Children travelling in the back may beg their parents to hire a bouncy castle, and if their birthday is coming up soon, you could get a booking. A company owner once told me that he would sometimes get a call on his mobile from the people driving behind him and they will ask him to pull over at the nearest lay-by so that they can discuss booking a bouncy castle with him. Now, that is powerful marketing!

If your van is currently not sign-written, it is a good idea to get *magnet signs*. One good booking and they are paid for!

A second tip is to advertise that you are a member of the BIHA literally EVERYWHERE! The BIHA logo gets him a lot of EXTRA work, and it will get you more work as well if you use it. This creates a really good impression with potential customers and affects the 'perception' of his hire company in the minds of people, as they trust him more.

Any inflatable hire company that does NOT display the BIHA logo on their business stationery, vans, website, etc., is literally leaving hundreds or even thousands of pounds per year on the table!

According to a MORI Poll, 77% of people looking to use the services of a local company are more likely to choose a company which is a member of a Trade Association or a professional body (such as the BIHA).
So, if you are a member of the BIHA (and follow the code of ethics), it is very strongly recommended that you display the BIHA logo on all your marketing materials, etc. It should get you more work!

BIHA Tip 13

Add a high-quality promotional video to your website's homepage. This can increase your bookings by up to 40% instantly! Using video as part of your marketing mix is vital for the simple reason that people respond better to video than to any other medium.

Many bouncy castle websites look like a 'silent movie from the 1920's', but adding a video with exciting sound-track can transform your site into a fully multimedia, fun experience for your website visitors and customers. In other words, it will make your website come ALIVE.

In addition, Google loves YouTube Videos (They *own* YouTube!) and, as a result, Google will tend to rank your website higher up in the Google rankings, as compared to your competitors who do not have a video on their website! Also, when your prospective customers watch the video, they tend to stay longer on the site. This reduces 'bounce rate' of your website, and Google will then tend to rank you even higher.

The BIHA can now create professionally-made videos for your website to increase your conversion rates overnight by up to 40% instantly! The price for producing one video starts at only £50 for a video of around 2 minutes duration. EACH VIDEO TAKES APPROX TWO HOURS TO CREATE - SO IT IS OUTSTANDING VALUE FOR MONEY!

BIHA Tip 14
This BIHA Tip is a little bit like marmite -you will either love it, or you will hate it!

Over the last few years, I have been collecting ideas to increase the 'TRUST FACTOR' of bouncy castle hire companies (in the eyes of their customers and prospects), so they get more bookings!
The logic behind this is very simple - the more your customers, potential customers, website visitors and referrals trust you, then the more likely you are to get bookings and referrals (including lucrative bookings from corporates and Local Authorities, etc.)

The tip will not only impress your customers/prospects, but can get you quickly noticed by your local community, and directly helps save lives. It revolves around a much-needed service that approximately 10% of the population do - giving blood.

If you give blood -take a selfie -including the needle and tubes, etc., and the nurse if she is happy about it. Even better -take some video on your mobile phone and upload it to YouTube! Then put the selfie and/or the video on your website and Facebook page, etc.

Think it is a bit unprofessional and pointless? Think again...

Giving blood is one of the most selfless acts that you can possibly do. Your customers and prospects will know that you will not have been paid for it and will impress the heck out of them. Subconsciously they will be deeply moved by your compassion for fellow human beings (A pint of blood you donate can save the lives of THREE people)

Whether they like it or not -they will see you as being incredibly caring, and even quite courageous (i.e. not afraid of the process because some people have a fear of needles!) Because they see you as being a caring human being -they are likely to trust you more!

This should convert into a greater likelihood of them wanting to hire your inflatables as opposed to your competitors (everything else being equal). I have given blood (quite a lot), and it is actually quite an enjoyable experience -Ask any blood donor you know! And they will tell you it is!

However, if you like the above idea but have a genuine fear of needles, then there are other ways that you can benefit from it to impress your customers (and help good causes). E.g. Get photographs or video of yourself doing a charity fun run. Getting involved in Foodbank or some other charitable organisation to help the poor. Visiting sick children at Great Ormond Street Children's Hospital or your local hospital.

Helping out with any charity that has a very strong local community following. Etc., etc., etc.

Do not forget to photograph or video yourself, and add the footage to your website and social media sites. You may even get a mention or a pic in your local press. Do not forget to wear your corporate shirt or sweatshirt, etc. With your company logo clearly displayed.

My view is that having photographs (e.g. a selfie) or video of needles coming out of your arms is one the most powerful ways to show your potential customers that you are a caring company, who likes to help the local community. They will think privately if XYZ hire company is prepared to turn up at the medical clinic to donate blood, and not get paid for it, then how much more likely are they to turn up for my party or event. I think I will book them. More importantly, they will just see you as being a caring company! Please try this idea -the worst that can happen is that you save the lives of THREE people.

BIHA Tip 15
Are you including an FAQ (Frequently Asked Questions) page on your website? If not, then you should! It will make your hire company look more professional, and it will REDUCE the number of QUESTIONS that your prospective customers will ask you.

In other words, it will free up your time, as you do not have to answer the same questions over and over again to your customers. Also, it is more content that Google can index and help push you higher up the rankings.

BIHA Tip 16
This tip concerns a complaint about a BIHA member from a customer who hired a rodeo bull. She posted a negative review on the member's Google+ page saying that she was outraged because she was asked to pay an extra fee because the party went on longer than planned.

Almost unbelievably, she also complained that the 2 men operating the rodeo bull were, "staring at her chest" while she was on it. A negative review of this nature can actually damage the reputation of a rodeo bull company, as potential customers can so easily find these negative reviews, and it can discourage them from booking.

Fortunately, the BIHA member did some damage limitation and responded to her negative review by saying that 1) It was clearly mentioned in the hire agreement that if the event went half an hour or more over the four hours, then an extra £40 would be payable. He explained that it was only fair that the 2 operators be paid extra for staying late.

With regards to, "staring at her chest" this was responded to by saying that the operators have to watch the riders on the bull like a hawk, so that in the event of a fall or problem, then the mechanical motion of the bull can be immediately stopped. He also went on to say that Health and Safety is of absolute importance to his company.

So, the upshot is that although the BIHA member found himself with a bad review, he was able to turn it around to put his company in a good light. It is really important that you check your customer reviews on Google+, Facebook, Twitter, etc., and if there are any negative ones - you need to 'nip them in the bud' before they start costing you bookings.

BIHA Tip 17
Some of your customers are so happy with your service that they are telling their family, friends and co-workers about you. In effect, they are 'cheerleaders' for your business. But do you know who they are??

How do you identify those customers and help them spread the good word about your service? You have made an impression on them, but what have you done for them lately? They say it is important to know who your friends are. But many hire businesses do not take the time to find out which customers are raving about them online and to their family, friends and acquaintances. And those companies lose out when they neglect these loyal customers.

Some of your most powerful marketing is in the hands of these people. Are you doing anything to recognize this great service they are performing for you? Sometimes, you will stumble upon these types of customers naturally and find that they cannot stop thanking you and telling others about your service.

They may even rave about you on Facebook and/or Twitter. When you find a customer like this, take really good care of them make sure you thank them often and offer them special deals, and special deals to the people to whom they refer you. After you have completed a hire booking, you may even want to put out a brief questionnaire asking your customer questions such as:

> "How likely are you to refer us to your family and friends on a scale of one to 10?". If the customer puts 9 or 10, then you know that you have a potential 'cheerleader' on your hands!

BIHA tip 18
Nowadays more and more companies are connecting with their customers, clients and even patients via text messaging. The reason for this is that it cuts through all the clutter of life like a knife. When I receive a text, I usually stop whatever I am doing (within reason) and read it -unless of course, I am driving or in a meeting.

E.g. On Friday, I received a text from my dentist confirming my appointment for a filling the following week. Also, my TV channel provider texted me to confirm that an engineer would be visiting my home to fix my TV fault. With smartphones, you can actually maintain a dialogue of text messages with your customers (very similar to the way that the threads and posts are organised on the discussion forum at www.BouncyCastleOwner.com)

You can use this to your advantage by developing a 'text relationship' with your customers using some or all of these:

1) A text to confirm the inflatable booking immediately after it has been made
2) A text message the night before the booking to remind them.
3) A text message DURING the booking to make sure everything is going well.
4) A text message to confirm collection time
5) Here is the clincher -a text message a day or two after the event to ask if they enjoyed having the bouncy castle and ask for any

feedback. (In other words, you are asking them for a review or testimonial). As you probably know, reviews are an extremely powerful way of getting new customers into your business, and also Google loves the fresh new content of reviews on your website.

Also, a year later you can text the customer again and ask them if they would like to re-book with your company. And, this is when the magic kicks in......

When you text your customer a year later (or sooner if they have several children) to remind them to book you, providing they have not deleted them, they should see all the text messages that were exchanged between them and you previously. Hopefully, if they see the review/feedback that they sent you a year (or less) previously, it will reinforce in their minds that you are the "go-to" bouncy castle hire company in their area. I.e. it will help create loyalty!

BIHA Tip 19
This excellent idea was actually shared with me by the caretaker of a very popular community centre in the town where I live.

She used to refer virtually all the inflatable hire bookings to me - whenever anyone used to hire her hall for a children's event - regardless of whether or not they had actually booked a castle. She actually went further than what most caretakers do! She recommended to the organiser that they book an inflatable if they had not already done so.

In other words - she did much of the selling for me!

Here is her advice applicable for all BIHA members who want more indoor work (during both peak and off-peak seasons). When you list on your website all the LOCAL community centres (and their contact details, etc.) that can accommodate bouncy castles, do not just list them all like a long 'shopping list' and expect your potential customers to ring them to check the facilities, etc. Instead, actually write down what each community centre can offer your customers and potential customers in detail.

FOR EXAMPLE: "Have you considered using the XYZ community centre in Birmingham? The XYZ Community Centre is absolutely ideal for holding children's and adult parties or any gathering requiring excellent indoor facilities. The centre is exceptionally well resourced with kitchen, (refrigerator, freezer, cooker, hob, microwave, wall-mounted drinks), hot water, cups, plates, jugs and a separate room for laying out food, tables and chairs with rooms dedicated for very young children's play areas, and parkland outside. As we serve the local community, we ensure that our rates are the lowest in the areas. Call Mary, the Caretaker on 0123456789." If you mention this on your website, you are serving two purposes: Firstly you are promoting the hall to people in your local area, which should please the hall owners/caretaker.

Secondly, you are educating your potential customers that they can hire a hall in the winter (or even all the year round) to accommodate your inflatables, and also enjoy excellent indoor facilities. A 'win-win' situation for everyone. As far as I know, not one member is using this approach to get more bookings in the off-peak months.

As an additional benefit - if you use the above example for all the LOCAL halls in your catchment area - you will be increasing the amount of content on your website. As you may know, Google likes lots of content on websites, and the more local it is, the better! Google rewards fresh, relevant content with higher rankings.

BIHA Tip 20
I have had many conversations with BIHA members over the years about their websites (and their social media presence), and I have noticed that some of them become obsessed with trying to get their website to the top of Google and getting the 'lion's share' of bookings in their local area.
This is fine and is to be encouraged. HOWEVER, one of the problems with having this approach is that sometimes highly effective 'OLD-SCHOOL' marketing methods are ignored or forgotten about. This is a big mistake as

old-school marketing can produce surprisingly good results, as good, if not better than social media and websites. It has worked well for over 100 years, and will continue to do so because your customers do not spend all their time online -and when they do go online to book an inflatable with you they often come face to face with your competition!

Here are ten examples of 'old school marketing' methods which often get ignored by inflatable hire companies:

1) Get some cheap colour stickers printed up of your inflatable hire business. Do not forget to include your logo and website address! Then give them to the party host to hand out to the children at the party. They then become a walking advertisement for your hire business. An interesting additional benefit to these stickers is that you use the words "children only" to (hopefully) prevent adults from bouncing on them.
E.g. Special Guest of the BIRTHDAY BOY/GIRL. Bouncy Castles are great fun for us. Children Only!!! Tel: 1234567890 yourwebsite.co.uk

2) If your customer is too busy to write you a review/testimonial or too shy for you to video them on your smartphone; ask them to ring your special telephone 'hotline', where they can record their review. You can then use a special telephone gadget to record their voice and put it on your website. Recordings of your customers praising your hire business are not as good as a video testimonial but much better than a written testimonial which can be falsified, and potential customers are aware of this. To see more details on this idea, please visit the discussion forum at www.BouncyCastleOwner.com

3) Place leaflets on car windscreens where parents of young parents are likely to congregate, e.g. Local sports centres.

4) Have you supplied an inflatable for a local charity event over the summer? Or for a special community celebration, sporting event or interest. The chances are that you have. If so, then write a press release and submit it to your local newspaper together with some good quality pictures. If the newspaper decides to print it -then you will get

free adverting for your business. In addition, you could keep the press cutting, scan it to your website and forever more have 'social proof' that you provided a bouncy castle for your local community. If you hate writing, get someone else to do it for you!

5) Create a rock-solid Unique Selling Proposition (USP) that separates you from your local competitors. E.g. Do you also provide mini-marquees if the weather is bad, or offer a face-painting service? Do you offer an entire party package? If so, *tell* your potential customers.

6) Build and maintain a database of current and POTENTIAL customers, and then contact that database when your diary is not as busy as you would like it to be. Perhaps offer a special 'end of summer' offer, where, for example, if they book a second inflatable from you -they pay half price.

7) Learn how to upsell your hire service so that you can offer other related services to your customers. E.g. McDonalds cashiers are trained to say, "Would you like fries with your order?" It should be no different with your hire business. You should always be asking your customer if they want more inflatables or garden games or face-painting, etc. If you forget to ask them, then you are leaving a great deal of money on the table.

8) Always be testing! Try to always MEASURE your marketing efforts. Ideally, you should always know the return on investment (ROI) of your marketing spend. E.g. if you spend £50 per month advertising your business in various local newsagent's shop windows and it creates an additional 15 bookings per month, that is fine. But if the same money spent on buying an advertisement in your local paper produces one booking a month on average -then pump more money into the former and less (or none) into the latter.

9) Always be asking happy customers for referrals. Send "thank you" cards and small gifts to customers who continually refer you to their friends. Consider holding a 'Customer Appreciation Event' where, for example, you set up some of your inflatables in a hall (at the end of the season) and invite your best customers as a "thank you" for the

referrals they have given you. Express gratitude for referrals and repeat business and the results may surprise you.

10) Consider cold-calling local companies in your town or city. Many of the bigger ones organise family fun days, charity events and team-building days, etc., and are often on the lookout for new ideas and inspiration. Inflatables are considered to be one of the highest forms of entertainment for families so you should get a fairly warm response when you call. Ask to speak to the Social Secretary or HR department. Corporate bookings can be very lucrative indeed, and I have known BIHA members get referrals resulting from of them worth thousands of pounds.

11) One of my favourite old-school marketing methods is 'Refrigerator Magnets'. Most people open their refrigerator door several times per day so will always see your hire business details. When they want to re-book or pass you onto a referral, they will not have to look very far! Try to make your refrigerator magnet as colourful as possible. I have heard of BIHA members who do it the low cost, DIY way. They get their business card, laminate it, and then stick a wafer-thin magnet to the back and give it to their customers as a refrigerator magnet.

To sum up this tip of the week, I am not saying for one second that you pull the plug on your website and your Facebook page, (That would be business suicide!) Instead, I am simply suggesting that you remember the old way of getting bookings and include some (or all) of them in your overall marketing mix. You just might see a big surge in extra bookings - something that was not possible from just your website and Facebook page alone!

BIHA Tip 21
Something that is rarely discussed on the forum is the problem of hot weather giving kids sunburn while they are on the castle all day long.
So if you want to impress your prospective customers, tell them that your castle has a sun-cover to protect their children from getting sunburn and also an over-sized rain-cover in addition, to ensure that rain does not stop play and the children still keep dry.

This should pleasantly surprise your potential customers, gain you extra credibility, and you are more likely to get the booking as compared to your competitors who do not have such a systematic approach to strong sunshine or rain.

BIHA Tip 22
When I talk to BIHA members, one of the points raised is how they are getting bookings. In the early years of the BIHA, members used to say, "the Yellow Pages" then a few years ago, it was mainly from their websites.

Nowadays, members are telling me that a significant proportion of their bookings come from Facebook and other social media sites, in addition to their own websites.

However, posting on Facebook, Google +, Twitter, Instagram, Linked In, etc., can be extremely time-consuming although it has been proven to help you streamline your marketing and help you get more bookings!

So, is there a tool which can automate this task? Happily, there is! It is called HOOTSUITE, and is free for up to 3 social media sites. Here is an 8-minute video which explains how to use it:

https://youtu.be/CfP_Av0NAwM

The website is at: https://hootsuite.com

BIHA Tip 23
One way to add interest to your website is to include a weather widget that shows current weather conditions where your customers are likely to hire inflatables from you. Most weather widgets are free and are easy to add to your website.

This is very easy to do, and one example (which I use) is the Met Office Widget. Alternatively, you can use: **www.accuweather.com** If you want to add a weather widget to your website -contact your webmaster, or if you manage your own site you should be able to do it yourself.

BIHA Tip 24

This BIHA tip centres around an 'add-on' service to inflatable-hire and looks at a couple of companies that provide GUEST APPEARANCES of the birthday child's favourite character (e.g. from Disney films)

This add-on service can command 'big money' as parents love to surprise their children with something very special on their big day. Darling Manor and Storybook Entertainment are two companies which offer the same type of service and who have both enjoyed such huge success that they have now joined forces.

They are an award-nominated, fully-insured, DBS-checked company, which "can't wait to add magic to your party or event!" They have a very important disclaimer that reads as follows: "Our characters are NOT name-brand copyrighted characters. Our characters are either generic or from the public domain. We can only accept bookings from individuals who are aware that we DO NOT represent any licensed characters. If you require a licensed, copyrighted character for your event, you should contact the company/copyright holders. Please DO NOT confuse our characters with any trademarked characters. Storybook Entertainment has no association with any other companies."

Instead of Snow White, they have a 'Poison Apple Princess', which is basically a woman dressed in a costume that looks a lot like Snow White's. Instead of Tinkerbell, they have 'Pixie'; instead of Ariel from The Little Mermaid, they have 'Mermaid Princess'; and instead of Sleeping Beauty, they have 'Sleeping Princess'. Apparently, their most in-demand characters currently are the sisters from Frozen, which are billed as the 'Snow Sisters'.

They basically acquire these costumes and hire local budding actresses (who have been DBS-checked) to wear them and send them to the actual birthday parties to make an appearance in character for a certain amount of the party's duration.

They are very popular and so successful that they are usually booked up months in advance. They are imminently even going to offer a venue for, the parties: up until now, they have had to make the trip to the venues of the parties in order to make the appearance. Now they are going to bring the party to them, and make more money in the process.

Storybook Entertainment and Darling Manor have built up their portfolio of characters and also offer additional extras, such as bringing themed cupcakes to the parties or offering to handle the party bags. With so many children's films to choose from, and more being released constantly, the scope is pretty endless!

BIHA Tip 25
There is an additional benefit of BIHA membership. Details of every BIHA member's hire business are being pinned onto a UK map (powered by Google) which is featured prominently on both www.biha.org.uk and also the sister site and forum at www.BouncyCastleOwner.com

This will have 3 main benefits for you and your businesses.

1) It will make it easier for your customers and prospective customers to find you.
2) It will be fairer! In the past companies at the top of the members' list had a slightly unfair advantage over companies listed at the bottom. Now, all hire companies in the same local area are in the 'same boat' as they can all be seen instantly.
3) When your business is pinned to the UK map, it is another factor which tells Google that you are a real live business and that they should rank you higher. When I populated this map over I discovered some well-established inflatable hire businesses had not yet been recognised by Google and were not even listed in the Google Places listings (Now Google + Local, or business listings)

BIHA Tip 26
Google My Business and Why Every Inflatable Hire Business Should Use It. While I have been building the BIHA members' map of the UK, I have discovered that many inflatable hire companies (including some very well established ones) are still invisible to Google in respect of Google Places.

You may be getting bookings from "word of mouth referrals" and Facebook, etc., but if you are invisible to Google, then you are probably leaving a great deal of money on the table. Once Google is aware of your business, it will market your business COMPLETELY FREE OF CHARGE! With no hidden costs.

Up until quite recently, it was all quite confusing. However, Google has recently made life much easier for local business owners with the launch of its exciting new tool, Google My Business. It combines Places for Business, Google Local and Google+ Business under one easy-to-use dashboard. Now, managing multiple Google accounts has never been simpler, and the marketing advantages for your hire business (or any other business you own) are endless.

Here is a quick summary of some of the services included:

Google+ (Google Plus): This is Google's answer to Facebook and is a social networking platform. You can share messages, photographs, videos and links to your followers, directly from the My Business page.

Reviews: Google has an entire review platform which gives businesses ratings based on their reviews. This is all manageable through the main page.

Google Analytics: You can very quickly and easily see all of your website's statistics right on your business dashboard.

Insights: Insights gives you vital information on your visibility, engagement and trends in the market.

Maps: Manage your businesses location and information available on Google maps. Also, see the BIHA map powered by Google at https://mapsengine.Google.com/map/viewer?mid=zbk4b55zWig4.ki62Nd O3zZE8&cid=mp&cv=NIiVepE-1OI.en. Is your hire business on there?

As mentioned earlier, this is all a free service. If you currently use Google Places for business or Google+ Pages to manage your online presence, you will already have been upgraded. Not only that but they are fine-tuning the

My Business platform for mobile use too, and it is available for both iOS and Android.

Ways That YOU Can Take Advantage of My Business Right Now and Quickly Overtake Your Competition. Be easily found on Google. Brand Awareness is vital for any business. How can you gain customers if people do not know who you are or what your product is? As a local business, you will know how hard it can be to get high rankings on Google, especially if you are in competition with bigger and more well-known brands.

So in order to create better brand awareness your first step would be to create an effective search engine optimisation (SEO) strategy to make your site more searchable on Google. Research has proven (and you probably know from your own personal experience) that 75% of Google users never scroll past the first page. This highlights how having a poor Google ranking can have a detrimental effect on your business and branding because potential customers will not be able to find you.

This is where Google My Business steps in. When you create a My Business account, fill out your information as thoroughly and accurately as you can. It will help your business to show up on Search, Maps and Google+. Remember to include information such as the location of your business, your opening times, contact information, website address and pictures of your business.

Ensure that the information you put on Google is the exact same information that you have on your website and any other places where your website is listed. Consistency is EXTREMELY important in SEO, and it can affect your ratings if there are any contradictions. The more information you add, the more Google's search algorithms will work to help with your own ranking.

Together, all of these features will give your customers an inside glimpse of your business and make it easier for them to make the decision to engage with you. As a result of doing this, when potential customers are searching specifically for your business or simply doing a broad search on business within your industry, they will be more likely to find your information and visit your website and book *you* rather than your competitors.

Connect with existing and potential customers As well as making your business easier to find in Google searches, you can also manage your Google+ page from your My Business dashboard. It has taken a while for people to get used to the Google+ social media, and most people still prefer and use Facebook and other social media sites but bear in mind that your Google+ business page gives a significant boost to your SEO and increases trust in your brand.

Google measures who comments, shares or +1's your post, then captures this information and identifies your audience's identity, activity and interests and then delivers your content in front of this demographic in organic search results.

The other advantage of using Google+ is this; while other social media sites place a, 'no follow' tag on any link you post, Google+ does not. So if you posted a link on Facebook, for example, any links that you put in your posts (to your website or special offers, etc.), they would not influence your business page ranking. Google, on the other hand, treats them as web pages which then helps increase your sites visibility and page rank.

But even without the SEO benefits, Google+ is also a good way to engage with your audience and build a long-term relationship with them which will make people trust your company more. We all know that people trust word of mouth recommendations, especially if it is from people whom they know. So when followers and customers are engaging with your content and are even in some cases re-posting it on their own pages, it will not take long for others to notice that you have a brand and reputation that can be trusted.

Just as on any other social media platform, if you expect any kind of results on Google+ you need to be consistent and post regularly. If you have a company blog, post the links on your page and ask your audience to read and share them. Post good quality pictures of your inflatables and other hire equipment so that your followers can get to know you better and have a clearer picture of who you are. It will encourage brand loyalty.

It is worth remembering that any content you share should be relevant and interesting to your audience. You do not want to keep posting promotional sales messages all the time. The point of Google+ is not to push your products or services on people but to create a close-knit community which will inspire trust and loyalty in your brand.

BIHA Tip 27
I need to explain that the following ideas are from the book called 'Influence' by Robert Cialdini (go grab it on Amazon), and he coined the phrase, "Weapons of influence." This post is my interpretation of how they can be applied to bouncy castle/play inflatable hire to get and retain more customers for you. The principles discussed can be applied to any product or service in virtually any niche.

Influence is probably the best business/sales/marketing book I have ever read, and Cialdini is a psychologist. These six "weapons" will set a strong psychological foundation for your marketing efforts and will make the potential customer comfortable with signing up with you by eliminating their uncertainty and persuading their subconscious to act in a certain way (the way you want them to act). You want to break down their wall by allaying their fears and objections to where they feel completely comfortable with paying for your hire services.

They are:
1. Reciprocation - I believe it builds a friendly trust that is absolutely necessary for any business relationship or transaction. This could be in the form of buying your potential client's product or service, offering them something free of charge (SEO, website, copywriting), sending them a new customer, doing them a simple favour, or offering them free advice, etc. The human psyche dictates that they will feel the need to 'return the favour' which works to your advantage. Reciprocation also takes you from being a stranger selling something to a friend.

2. Commitment and Consistency - Stay committed to meeting the client's goals and getting them more customers, and be consistent by keeping promises, honouring agreements, backing-up claims and statements, etc. If you say you are going to follow up with them, do it. A year later, you want them thinking you are still helping them as much as you were when they started paying you. I suppose this is rather obvious, but I have seen that people tend to get lazy and throw consistency out the window when they take things for granted once they have acquired the client. If you do not keep your word, why should anyone trust you? Without trust, they will not feel comfortable buying from you.

3. Social Proof - As I have also said before, referrals are probably the most powerful marketing tool out there. A direct referral from a friend provides significant social proof from a third party that you can do what you claim. Testimonials are similar in that they are evidence that you can indeed provide a valuable service that benefits the potential client who may be sceptical about what you are selling. If you can show a portfolio of websites you have built or ranked, or sales copy you have written, do it. All these things allay the potential client's fears, apprehensions, and delusions. Without some form of evidence or proof, the potential client will subconsciously feel they are taking a risk. We want to mitigate that perceived risk.

4. Liking - Often overlooked, the likeability factor is important in any relationship or transaction. The potential client does not have to agree with your values or subscribe to your moral code, but they have to 'like' you at least on a very basic level. No one wants to do business with a 'snobby' mean person, so put a smile on and just be friendly. This also fits in with reciprocation in that doing them a favour will subconsciously cause them to like you and see you more as a friend rather than a salesman. If you spilt coffee on your shirt that morning, do not let it get you in a bad mood right before meeting with a client. Clear your head of any angry thoughts and be a generally nice person. This seems like common sense I know, but really think about it the next time you walk into a meeting.

5. Authority - I consider authority to be 'expert status'. Note that this does not mean you have actually to be an expert, you just have to appear to be. Those are two completely different things. As I have said before, people will perceive you to be an expert simply because you know a little more than they do on a particular subject. Chances are you will know much more about internet marketing services than the potential client, so you are already good there. Establish yourself as a seeming authority in your market, and you will become the go-to person for the sorts of things you offer. Be the expert, but do not get so technical that you talk down to them. You do not want the client to feel inferior. Remember, be their friend, just make it evident that you know what you are talking about and that they need your assistance. I believe authority comes with experience, so this one will automatically be taken care of overtime in most cases.

6. Scarcity - Scarcity generates demand. It does not even have to be real. Perceived scarcity works the same way - the human mind cannot tell the difference between reality and imagination. Making your product or service exclusive in some way makes the potential client want to grab onto it sooner rather than later. Exclusivity also allows you to charge more. A perfect example here is doing SEO for lawyers. Every lawyer I have dealt with has their specific targeted area of law (DUI, personal injury, criminal defence, etc.) and obviously does not want you to offer the same services to their direct competition. I tell them that is fine, but it is going to cost them much more for a non-compete agreement. They usually understand that anyway and are happy to pay for it.

BIHA Tip 28
Are you trying to design a really eye-catching flyer for your hire business but need some help and inspiration??

Go into Google.co.uk and in the search box type out "bouncy castle advertisement." Then click on IMAGES. You will get a huge number of bouncy castle images INCLUDING advertisements that other companies have used. It goes without saying that you should not copy these advertisements, but there is nothing to stop you from using some of the ideas.

Some of the flyer designs are quite spectacular. Getting your flyers organised now, or giving them a make-over will put you in a good position for next years' season.

BIHA Tip 29
Are you DBS checked? The good news is that you do not have to be to hire out inflatables - because you are not directly working with children and vulnerable adults. HOWEVER, a BIHA member rang me up last week, and we discussed the whole issue of DBS checks for inflatable hire companies. The upshot was that we both agreed that being DBS-checked was (at the very least) a valuable marketing tool. In other words, if a prospective customer sees that a hire company they are thinking of using is DBS checked then they are more likely to choose them as opposed to another local hire company which is not DBS-checked.(Everything else being equal).

BIHA Tip 30
I really like this 'old-school' marketing idea, and you WILL take extra bookings and make more money if you act on this. When you hire an inflatable to your customers - do you hand them out a business card and flyers to give to their friends and neighbours? Most hire companies do. But do you also give your customers a refrigerator magnet for them to attach to their refrigerator and freezer so that they see your hire company every day! I expect very few do this.

Ask your local print company to turn some of your business cards into magnets. The cost should be quite low - especially if they already have the artwork design for your cards in their system. Typical costs tend to be around 10p - 30p per card magnet depending on where you go. If your customers hand out a few of these business cards to their friends and they also stick them to the door of their refrigerators, then you are getting a lot of very cheap and virtually permanent advertising.

If you action this refrigerator magnet business card idea, try to use Tip 28 above and get the very best eye-catching design that you can. Use very bright colours and fonts, etc., and even get your best bouncy castle printed on the magnet.

BIHA Tip 31
Everybody talks about it as a quick way to grow their inflatable hire businesses, but virtually no-one does it! However, for thousands of years, it has been the most POWERFUL and EASIEST method of getting new customers into your business. If done properly, then it can grow your business beyond your wildest dreams!

I am talking about the power of getting referrals which has been touched upon several times before at the BIHA, but in this 'BIHA Tip of the Week' there is an added twist to it which puts the whole process on steroids!
When you deliver and set up an inflatable - do you get gasps of excitement from the customer and their children? I used to, and it always gave me a thrill! Do your customers sometimes just stand there in awe admiring the artwork, etc., while their children are running around in a frenzy of anticipation for their 'favourite activity'?

This is precisely the time when it is a good idea to ask your customer for a referral or two. E.g. Customer: "That is a stunning bouncy castle, and the artwork is amazing!"

You: "I'm really glad you like it. My business works very much on a LOCAL referral basis, and I try to invest in the best quality bouncy castles rather than spend a small fortune each year on advertising. Do you have any neighbours in your street who have youngsters and may be interested in hiring a bouncy castle or another inflatable?"

You: (Keep quiet at this point to let your customer answer!)

Customer: "Yes, Mr and Mrs Smith three doors down have four young children, and they are always having parties at home."

You: "Are you OK if I drop them a quick note just to let them know that you used me today?"

Customer: "Yes, that's fine, I'm happy to recommend you, since you have provided a great service, and the children are more than happy!"

You: "Thanks for that, it's much appreciated. Do you have any other neighbours who may be interested?"

Customer: "Yes, Fred Brown opposite us has two young children. He would also be interested. My brother will be along later, and he also has young children, I'll give him your business card (or flyer)."

You: "Thanks so much for those three referrals; I will drop off a quick note later to your neighbours. (OPTIONAL) As a token of my appreciation - here's a £5 coupon off your next hire, and a coupon and business card for your brother."

Now, this is where the 'magic' happens, and I have never heard anyone do this before. You have a prepared letter which says something like this...

> Dear Mr and Mrs Smith,
>
> My name is xxxxxxxxx. I have just delivered a bouncy castle to Mr and Mrs Green, your neighbours at Number 26 earlier today.
>
> You may even see or hear some very excited children on it during the course of today. Your own children may even be guests there!
> They all love the bouncy castle and if you are interested in having one for your child's next birthday - please call me on xxxxxxxxxxx
>
> You can see pictures of them at my website here xxxxxxxxxx
> I look forward to being of service to you sometime in the future.
>
> Best wishes
>
> Xxxxxxxxx
>
> P.S. All our bouncy castles have rain-covers to keep the children dry in the event of showers, and they also act as sun covers as well.
>
> P.P.S. Bouncy castles are one of the best ways of entertaining a group of children and take away a great deal of the hassle and headache of organising and running a children's party. Our prices start at just £50 per day.
>
> P.P.P.S. We pride ourselves in only providing clean and high-quality bouncy castles, so your children have maximum enjoyment, and will remember the experience for years to come.

Can you see the power of this little note?

If you have a few of these notes already pre-printed in your van, you just have to spend 2 minutes filling out the blanks and delivering it to the neighbours' houses. They are precisely targeted, and you are saving on the cost of buying stamps and envelopes, etc.

BEST OF ALL: It is 'social proof' from a personal recommendation, which they know, trust and are likely to be friends with. The psychology behind this is extremely powerful! You are no longer a stranger to them, but are virtually a friend of a friend! They won't know you, but they will feel that they almost do!

- If time permits and you can deliver the letter personally, then the effect could be even stronger.
- Some of your customers may be more than happy to mention virtually EVERYBODY down their street who has young children. You may be able to post 5, 10 even 15 of these little notes - and it can be an absolute 'game-changer' for your hire business!
- If you run another service-type business alongside your inflatable hire business, such as landscape-gardening, face-painting, gutter-cleaning, child-minding, handyman/woman, oven-cleaning, marquee-hire, dog-walker, children's entertainer, etc., then you can also use this idea to GROW your businesses extremely quickly.

Tips Shared By The BIHA

These are somewhat random, but there is gold in these tips from established members of the BIHA.

- ALWAYS take payment on delivery. This stops customers trying to wriggle out of paying at the end of the party. To counter the excuse of, "We haven't got any cash in the house" take along your PDQ machine and swipe their debit or credit card. It is guaranteed payment.

- Make sure everything you hire out to your customers is really CLEAN and in tip-top condition - including your crash-mats! 'Cowboys' tend to put out old and dirty castles which gives the industry a bad name. The cleaner your equipment is the more referrals you will get!

   There is one exception though - when I deliver castles to a local pub where I know it will probably be abused - I do not rent them my best and cleanest units!

- Always be really happy, friendly and nice to customers whatever the situation. They will remember you for this, and be much more likely to book you again.

- Charge more for your inflatable hire! Many hire companies are too cheap, way too cheap! If you charge more money, then you will get better quality customers who will think that you are more reliable.

- Cheaper companies tend to pick up the lower quality customers, while I pick up premium customers because I charge more.

   As a BCN (www.bouncycastlenetwork.com) member, I have found their online booking system a major success in helping me run the day to day business of hiring. I would recommend their services to anyone.

- Manners cost nothing! Be polite and courteous at all times with customers, suppliers, etc.

- Get the BIHA to help optimize your website and start getting it ranking high up in the search engines. Do not leave it to chance or guesswork - get the BIHA to help you. It's very affordable!

  Everything is online now, and a major part of our success is down to the splendid people at the BCN (Bouncy Castle Network www.bouncycastlenetwork.com). They really give us the tools needed to run our business and booking site. If you are not currently with them, you are really missing out!

- On all overnight hires, we charge the hirer £20 cash refundable deposit. This money is refunded on collection with the equipment returned clean and in the same condition delivered. It really works, and we have never had a customer refuse to pay.

- Get a website with BCN; it is the best thing we have done.

  Get an A-Frame Board and stick a poster of your business and contact numbers to it when supplying castles to events. You will not believe the amount of extra work that you get from it.

- Get some Tee-Shirts from Vista Print, with your company name, logo, website and phone number on them, and then wear them everywhere you go.

- Network with other local bouncy castle hire companies that are reputable rather than be enemies.

- Try the new Google Earth. No downloads needed. It runs on the web and will work on your desktop, tablet or phone.

  You can find it at **https://earth.google.com/web/**

  When you get there, click the 'fly to location' icon in the lower right of the screen (it's next to the little man icon).

  After the screen zooms in, hold down your shift key and scroll your mouse up down and left and right.

  I think you will be impressed with what you see. Google Earth is an extremely useful tool to be able to check out the area where your inflatable will be sited. (E.g. the size of the customer's back garden) without the need to necessarily do a site inspection.

- Before paying fees to self-appointed 'training instructors' check them out first. Speak to others who have attended their training courses, get their feedback and opinions. Go onto the forum at www.BouncyCastleOwner.com and ask people what they thought of these courses. Check with the course organiser that they have a proper sound system in place (e.g. microphone and speakers) to ensure that the noise of the castle fan does not make it difficult to hear the speaker.

- If you receive an email from a customer - never assume that they have read your reply. It may have ended up in their spam or junk mail folder or just got lost! Go ahead and phone them. You can then make sure they have received your email and/or encourage them to book with you if they are undecided or procrastinating.

- Always promote your hire business on the BACK of your van. You will get work from cars following behind (This tip is featured in more detail above).

- Get friendly with other inflatable hire companies in your local area. Take them out for a coffee or a pub meal, etc. Pass bookings and referrals to each other. If you make enemies of your competitors, then you will all lose out. There is more than enough work in most towns and cities to go round.

  I am not geared up to take last minute bookings - so I can pass these on to my competitors who can take on this kind of work.

  Do not try and take on all of the work yourself. Use drivers to do it for you. We have 5 staff who deliver and collect the castles for us.

- Take great photographs of all your hire products and show them off everywhere - let them do the selling for you!

- When you get a website built - make sure that it also includes SEO to help get your website ranked at the top of the search engines.

- I strongly recommend that you use your Facebook page to get bookings. However, I have noticed that the cancellation rate when customers book me via Facebook is higher than if they book through my website.

I am not sure of the reason behind this, but what I now do is that if a customer enquires through Facebook, I direct them to my website and my new booking system (run by Bouncy Castle Network) In addition, when a customer books via Facebook, I give them a discount code (worth £5 or £10) off the hire price.

To redeem this discount code, they need to:

a) Like and share my Facebook Page and
b) Book online via my website.

Once the customer has conformed to these two requirements, they get their discount of up to £10. The benefit to me: Not only do I get countless referrals as details of my company spread like wildfire through their friends' Facebook pages, etc., but also I get far fewer cancellations.

- Try to roll up your inflatables so that they are long and thin instead of short and fat. This will make it much easier for you to wheel them through gates and narrow garden side passages.

Also, the risk of scuffing or a rip is reduced.

- Try to keep some castles strictly for INDOOR USE ONLY. This will help keep them cleaner and newer for much longer. This can lead to happier customers and more referrals. Likewise, try to keep some units for OUTDOOR use only.

This rule sometimes gets broken during really busy peak times in the summer, and also where a customer wants an indoor hire at the last minute (e.g. if the forecast has turned bad)

- Join the BIHA, TIPE, and Bouncy Castle Network, and display their logos on everything you use to promote your business! This will guarantee you more work; because customers trust these logos even though they might not have a clue what they actually mean!

In their eyes, it means that you are following best practice, similar to CORGI for gas engineers (when the scheme ran, now Gas Safe Register, who knows that?) People did not know what CORGI meant let alone stood for, yet they trusted it. Likewise, customers trust the BIHA, TIPE, Bouncy Castle Network logos as having a mark of authority.

- Blacklist customers who give you bad reviews. (especially where their review is unjustified). They do not realise the potential damage that they are doing to your reputation.

- Join as many Facebook groups as you can, i.e. the BIHA group, as I have been picking up a lot of great hints and tips from there.

  Be aware that if you primarily use Facebook to get bookings - then you may get messed about by people wanting a big discount. Also, it is easy to get side-tracked into constant PM'ing with potential customers who can take up a great deal of your time. You want affluent customers and less management and interaction taking the booking.

- When you purchase your leads, consider getting an inline RCD. It helps to make sure you always have an RCD on the plug, so you do not forget them, plus it is easier for the outside garden type grey box terminals that do not allow for the large RCD fitting to connect. If you do get an in-line RCD, have it close to the male end, approx 3 foot from the end. Too close causes issues when it goes through windows.

- Yes, provide a really good service to your customers, and then you will AUTOMATICALLY develop a good reputation. Once you develop a good reputation, the referrals will flood in, and then there is no need to price-match.

- If your customer tells you that they can get a castle or mascot £10 - £20 cheaper elsewhere, be honest with the customer and tell them that there is probably a good reason why it is so much cheaper (e.g. it might not turn up on the day, or might not have a test certificate, or be dirty, and please do not ring me when your castle has not arrived, as I will be fully booked.)

  Make the customer aware that if they go for the very cheapest company, then there could be problems! Hold to your prices, be creative, but be professional at the same time and never directly slag off your competitors. Focus on providing an exceptionally good service that your cheap competitors just cannot match - because they are too cheap!

- Work EXTREMELY closely with your reputable local competitors - it can grow your business beyond your dreams!

   Use Facebook to help get you bookings - it really does work well!

USEFUL INDUSTRY LINKS

Here are some web links that you may find useful for your bouncy castle hire business.

www.biha.org.uk British Inflatable Hirers Alliance (BIHA).

www.facebook.com/groups/biha4u BIHA Facebook Group for the industry.

www.facebook.com/groups/359906244348902/ BIHA Facebook Group for members-only.

www.BouncyCastleOwner.com BouncyCastleOwner.com Discussion forum and sister site of the BIHA.

www.CustomerTopUp.com Customer Top Up (The Author's website marketing and SEO Agency).

www.bouncycastlebook.co.uk Compendium of bouncy castle hire profit books published by the BIHA.

www.seogym.co.uk The Author's SEO Agency Website.

www.pipa.org.uk PIPA Scheme.

http://rpii-inspectors.com RPII

www.playinspectors.com RPII

www.rospa.com Royal Society for the Prevention of Accidents (RoSPA).

www.naih.org.uk/info49.pdf Summary of en 14960 Standard.

www.companieshouse.gov.uk Companies House.

www.tipe.co.uk The Inflatable Play Enterprise.

www.bouncycastlenetwork.com Bouncy Castle Network (BCN).

www.hse.gov.uk/entertainment/fairgrounds/inflatables.htm HSE document on Bouncy Castles and other Play Inflatables.

http://www.biha.org.uk/about-the-biha/manufacturers/ A selection of manufacturers of inflatables.

www.brightfbs.co.uk Bright Future Business Solutions. Embroidery, graphic design, flyers and much more.

https://www.gov.uk/browse/business Government site on help with starting a small business.

www.hse.gov.uk/legislation/hswa.htm More details of the Health and Safety at Work Act 1974.

www.hse.gov.uk/pubns/indg291.pdf Outline of PUWER REGS 1998.

www.hse.gov.uk/risk/ HSE Risk Management Guide.

www.hse.gov.uk/pubns/indg163.pdf HSE Guide to Risk Assessment.

Insurance Links:

a) **www.leisureinsure.co.uk** Leisureinsure

b) **www.fml-insurance.co.uk** FML Insurance

c) **www.peacockinsurance.co.uk** Peacock Insurance

d) **www.gmisl.co.uk** GS Imber Insurance

e) **www.bridleinsurance.co.uk** Bridle Insurance

f) **www.parkinsurance.co.uk** Park Insurance

g) **www.insursec.co.uk** Insurance Risk Management

In Closing

I sincerely hope that you have enjoyed reading this book and that it has informed you about starting and running a profitable bouncy castle hire business.

Whilst being edited it was brought to my attention that there is some degree of repetition. However, I decided to allow the repetition to remain inside the book because it covers extremely important areas of the business (e.g. health and safety), and I believe that by mentioning it more than once, the reader is more likely to act upon it and to make more money, and run a safer hire business as a direct result.

Don't make the mistake though of thinking that you can earn a huge income off hiring inflatables without doing any work! This industry can be fantastically rewarding, and extremely enjoyable to work in, but you do have to put in the work - especially at the weekends! Although once your cash-flow is healthy you can start to hire drivers and other staff which will massively ease your work-load. So, if after reading this book, you still think that you've got what it takes to run a successful and safe bouncy castle hire business then go for it! We at the BIHA (**www.biha.org.uk**) will always be here to help you.

We wish you every happiness and success in your new business venture.

Volume 2 is called 'Internet Marketing for Bouncy Castle Hire Companies -How to Double or Triple Your Bookings and Profits Using the Power of the Internet'.
www.bouncycastlebook.co.uk

BIHA Membership Benefits

Here are some of the main benefits of BIHA membership...

1) Access to a lively BIHA Facebook Group with approx. 2,700 members - see: **www.facebook.com/groups/biha4u**

1a) Access to a brand new BIHA members Facebook Group - (Just launched)
See: **https://www.facebook.com/groups/359906244348902/**

The BIHA 'Tip of the Week' is posted in this second BIHA Facebook Group.

2) Access to a discussion forum at **www.BouncyCastleOwner.com** (Please note that this once very lively forum has now been all but replaced by the BIHA Facebook Group but there are still over 41,000 posts on it going back to 2008).

3) Access to numerous profit tips, strategies and ideas, etc., in the "members-only" area of **www.biha.org.uk** and on **www.BouncyCastleOwner.com** to help you increase cash-flow, turnover and profits in your hire business, and improve enjoyment and fun, etc.

4) Numerous Safety tips -the provision of a 'Code of Ethics' at **www.biha.org.uk/code-of-ethics** to help educate customers towards safety.

5) Full permission to use the BIHA logo on your website, business cards, flyers, vans, uniforms and other marketing materials. This will help you attract more customers because it is a 'TRUST BADGE'. The more your potential customers trust your website, etc., then, the more bookings you should get -FACT!

6) Articles to help you TRANSFORM your inflatable hire business - e.g. see:
http://www.bouncycastleowner.com/public/department151.cfm

7) Get your hire business listed on THREE national online bouncy castle hire directories including a valuable BACK-LINK to your own website. (This helps improve your Google rankings!)

    a) Google Map See:

    https://www.google.com/maps/d/viewer?mid=zbk4b55zWig4.ki62NdO3zZE8

    b) BIHA online members directory. See:

    http://www.biha.org.uk/member-directory/

    c) See www.BouncyCastleHireUK.com (BIHA sister site and premier directory of members)

8) Discounts on your public liability insurance premiums of up to 30% with **www.leisureinsure.co.uk** (You just need to quote your BIHA membership number on their online quotation form).

9) Occasional newsletters and alerts via email - including the popular 'Spotlight on an Inflatable Hire Company', e.g.
http://www.bouncycastleowner.com/public/department184.cfm
and also:
http://www.bouncycastleowner.com/public/department187.cfm

10) A heavily subsidised FREE professional website (worth £1,000+) for your inflatable hire business if you need one. (E.g. **www.bouncebuddieswakefield.co.uk**) which also includes an online booking system (optional), and SEO to get your website ranking well in Google. (Conditions apply).

11) We also offer an extremely low-cost 'stand-alone' SEO service to get your website to the top of GOOGLE for your town or local area. (This is on a first-come-first-served basis)

12) You can also download essential documents and templates, e.g. Risk Assessments, Disclaimers, Terms and Conditions of Hire, Method Statements, Safety Cartoon Sheets, Invoice Templates, etc.

13) We can also create a FREE (or low-cost) promotional video for your hire business.

14) In the unlikely event of an insurance claim, the BIHA may be able to assist you.

15) In 2004, (when PLI was very expensive) the BIHA was solely responsible for locating a low-cost PL insurance provider which reduced PLI premiums by nearly 50% ACROSS THE WHOLE INDUSTRY, not just for BIHA members!

16) BIHA Van stickers (A4 size) which are just £2 each.

17) ENTERTAINMENT - Although safety awareness and profit tips are extremely important, the BIHA also has a strong entertainment element to it.

18) Access to me (Mark Jerram). I have 25 years' experience in the inflatable-hire industry and in addition, I am an award-winning SEO consultant, and can help you get your website to the top of Google (if this interests you, depending on availability of your town or city). A highly ranked website in Google = More bookings for you!

19) It's a basic human need to be part of an organisation that is bigger than ourselves. Running an inflatable hire business can be quite lonely. However, with the BIHA, because you are connecting with 'like-minded people', you can never be alone! You can make new friends, bounce ideas off other people, or just go onto the Facebook Group for a chat!

20) There are always opportunities to buy and sell used inflatables and accessories, etc., from other members.

21) Discounts with various manufacturers (e.g. Gala Tent are offering a 10% discount on their marquees and party tents to BIHA members).

22) Very large discounts on Yellow Pages advertising via their 'Corporate Advertising Scheme' (CAS). E.g. instead of paying approximately £300 per year for an advertisement you pay approximately £70 instead.

23) We also offer FREE legal advice via third party solicitors.

24) How to reduce your marketing costs, but get more customers for you at the same time (Our proprietary method). Also see: **www.customertopup.com**

25) Savings on fuel prices at the forecourts of up to 10p per litre.

All these membership benefits for under 75p per week, and you get full tax relief. It's an amazing return on your investment!

Please also see some reviews of the BIHA at:
http://www.biha.org.uk/written-reviews
and some video reviews at **www.biha.org.uk/video-reviews**

www.biha.org.uk

www.facebook.com/groups/biha4u (BIHA Facebook Group)

www.facebook.com/groups/359906244348902/ (BIHA 'Members Only' Facebook Group)

www.BouncyCastleOwner.com (PRIVATE discussion forum for the inflatable hire industry)

www.seogym.co.uk Get more customers into your hire business by getting to the top of the Search Engines (Search Engine Optimization - SEO)

www.bouncycastlebook.co.uk Compendium of bouncy castle hire profit books published by the BIHA

Printed in Great Britain
by Amazon